"'Grow old along with me,' Robert Browning invited us. Not a bad enticement. Aging is a journey of glory; wrinkles can be either ruts of despair or channels of significance. David Petty wants us to be conquistadors claiming the land where the flag of our mature significance must be planted."

> — *Calvin Miller*
> Professor of Preaching
> and Pastoral Ministries,
> Beeson Divinity School

"There are aspects of aging that are often overlooked by senior Americans. In *Aging Gracefully: Keeping the Joy in the Journey,* sociologist David Petty has compiled an inspiring guidebook on every aspect of elderhood from his lifetime of teaching university courses on gerontology. This volume includes research gleanings, stories from senior adults in the midst of life adjustments, quotations from the Scriptures, and helpful observations from the author's own life. Dr. Petty provides wisdom and spiritual guidance for the elderly and their caregivers in this inspiring overview of the aging process."

> — *C. W. Brister*
> Distinguished
> Professor Emeritus
> of Pastoral Ministry,
> Southwestern Baptist
> Theological Seminary

AGING
GRACEFULLY

AGING
GRACEFULLY

KEEPING THE JOY IN THE JOURNEY

DAVID L. PETTY

BROADMAN
&HOLMAN
PUBLISHERS

NASHVILLE, TENNESSEE

0-8054-2690-6

Published by Broadman & Holman Publishers,
Nashville, Tennessee

Dewey Decimal Classification: 305.26
Subject Heading: AGING \ ELDERLY \ OLD AGE

Unless otherwise stated all Scripture citation is from the
Holy Bible, New International Version, © 1973, 1978,
1984 by International Bible Society. Also quoted is *The
Message,* the New Testament in Contemporary English,
© 1993 by Eugene H. Peterson, published by NavPress,
Colorado Springs, Colo.

1 2 3 4 5 6 7 8 9 10 07 06 05 04 03

To God's wonderful senior saints,
who have challenged and inspired me in the faith,
have trusted his Son to the end, and
are waiting their turns to greet him in eternity.

I salute you and thank you!

CONTENTS

ACKNOWLEDGMENTS

Since retiring five years ago, I have wondered how a professional gerontologist might bring pertinent information along with an encouraging word to readers who are concerned about their aging experiences. As I became convinced that such could be a worthy goal, I spoke to Gary Terashita, and he agreed to become my editor. I am indeed grateful for his faith and encouragement in helping make this dream a reality.

Through many years my mother and my late father have supported my work as student and teacher as I responded to God's calling. Such support and encouragement have been a genuine blessing for me.

My three sons, David Jr., Joel, and Jason, are inspirations to me. Because I have fatherly pride in their work and, particularly, in their pursuit of integrity and excellence in life, I have felt much freedom to work at my calling with the knowledge that they are following God as he leads.

Deanna, my wife of forty-two years, is a wonderful *ezer* (helper). I hope I am the same, in the masculine sense, for her. She often (jokingly, I think) takes credit for me; in reality, much credit is due her! I am grateful to God for our life together!

I am thankful for many of God's faithful who have gone before me. They are among the "great cloud of witnesses" who surround us (Heb. 12:1). May God be praised for all these lovely gifts and remembrances!

INTRODUCTION

Life is a wonderful odyssey, an incredible journey. I call it wonderful because for each of us it starts not by accident but by God's design. David, king of Israel, said it this way:

> For you created my inmost being;
>   you knit me together in my mother's womb.
> I praise you because I am fearfully and
>   wonderfully made;
>   your works are wonderful,
>   I know that full well.
> My frame was not hidden from you
>   when I was made in the secret place.
> When I was woven together in the
>   depths of the earth,
>   your eyes saw my unformed body.
> All the days ordained for me
>   were written in your book
>   before one of them came to be. (Ps. 139:13–16)

Isaiah understood King David when he wrote:

Listen to me, you islands;
hear this you distant nations:
Before I was born the LORD called me;
    from my birth he has made mention of my name.
He made my mouth like a sharpened sword,
    in the shadow of his hand he hid me;
he made me into a polished arrow
    and concealed me in his quiver. (Isa. 49:1–2)

Life is also a pilgrimage, a journey with a special purpose. Christians understand that a pilgrimage represents change over time: as we live our lives, our purpose is to mature in Christ, to grow in his grace, and to press toward the goal of becoming perfect in him. This last phrase prefaces the idea written by Paul to the Christians at Philippi: "Forgetting what is behind and straining toward what is ahead, I press on toward the goal to win the prize for which God has called me heavenward in Christ Jesus"(Phil. 3:13b–14).

Life as odyssey and pilgrimage suggests positive, profound experiences, though we all recognize that life in an imperfect world is fraught with difficulties, trials, and tests of our faith. The Lord Jesus Christ told us it would be that way; and, of course, it is.

I am undertaking this bit of writing to encourage you in the later stages of your life. As I grow old along with you, I look forward to what lies ahead. It will be an exciting adventure (if I want it to be), and it will have purpose (if I allow God to have his way in my life). God has provided the raw materials—the earth on which we live and the natural laws that govern it; the rules of play (his eternal standards); and human volition (freedom to live and choose and become). Even so, we have a large responsibility—for accurate knowledge, appropriate attitudes, and correct behavior.

As you read the following chapters, I invite you to get in touch with the aging process and the reality of your own aging. Then ask yourself these questions: Who do I want to be? and What do I want to do for the rest of my life?

Chapter One
AGING: CHANGE AND ADJUSTMENT

We all are growing older—one day at a time. Beyond this statement of similarity, I know of little else that holds true for all elderly people—or people of any other age group.

Most of us give scant recognition to the aging process until we begin to notice physical changes: a wrinkle in the corner of the eye or mouth, a gray hair in the head or eyebrow, an "age" spot on the back of the hand, or some other common indicator. When one or more of these "symptoms" appear, our responses range from quiet resignation to full-blown panic. So, how are *you* dealing with the fact of *your* aging?

Aging is a process of change; it is both inevitable and irresistible. If we wish to enjoy the later part of life (or any other part for that matter), we must learn to adapt to the changes that come our way. My view is that the human organism is highly resilient in its makeup (physically, emotionally, socially, etc.) and thus quite capable of adjusting successfully to change. Let's consider three basic dimensions of change associated with aging. A fourth dimension, the spiritual, will be addressed later.

THE PHYSIOLOGICAL DIMENSION

The most obvious aging changes are physiological. Physical changes are well documented and are the ones most often cited in developing and perpetuating stereotypes of the aged. Let me describe some of my own physical changes. I am in my sixty-sixth year; the top of my head is bald; the hair on the sides and back of my head is light brown slowly turning gray. While my weight is good relative to my height and age, my face is thin and somewhat gaunt looking. A noticeable dewlap sags between my chin and throat. A couple of wrinkles just south of each corner of my mouth are becoming increasingly prominent, but they disappear when I smile. (I try to smile a lot!)

I wear eyeglasses to correct presbyopia (farsightedness). At age forty I secured my first pair—half-lens reading glasses—which I wore only when reading. Several years later, however, the optometrist added some correction to my distant range of vision because I had discovered this need to pass the eye exam to renew my driver's license. You guessed it; I've been in bifocals ever since!

Now, will you analyze this brief self-description with me? (I'll try to be objective!) A balding pate, wrinkles in my face, and vision needing correction are all changes that have happened. As far as I can tell, there is little or nothing I could have done to negate or even slow those changes. What I have done is adjust to them, with few discouraging words or thoughts. My philosophy? Why think negatively or pessimistically about inevitable (for me) changes? As I see it, God still has the hairs on my head numbered—now he just has fewer to count!

On the other hand, my gaunt facial features may be due, in part, to my losing ten to twenty pounds of excess fat about thirty years ago. I was responsible for that. My philosophy? Having a good weight (175 pounds) relative to my height (seventy-one inches) and age (sixty-five years) is worth working for, and if getting a thin look to my facial features (and that dratted dewlap) goes with that change, so be it! Successful adaptation to aging requires acting to *change what you can change for the better and not worrying about those things over which you have no control.*

I began playing racquetball thirty-two years ago at age thirty-three. Previously I had played a little tennis, handball, and squash; but after trying racquetball, it seemed to be the game for me. I developed a game of power, and I was quick enough to play a fairly decent game. By carefully selecting my opponents, I became successful on the racquetball court.

During these ensuing thirty-two years, I have slowed down significantly. But have I given up racquetball? No! I have abandoned the power game and have replaced it with a game of finesse. I still enjoy the competition, I still enjoy success often enough, and I still get the needed exercise that, coupled with good nutrition, helps me keep my weight at a good level.

To have given up racquetball would, for me, have been an unsuccessful outcome. To adjust my game to accommodate my aging changes has been a much better solution.

The Psychological Dimension

Psychological changes also accompany the aging process. The one change that seems to concern people most often has to do with their memory. Have you noticed how many jokes folks tell about memory lapses? For the most part, I think it helps us to poke fun at our own frailties, and some of these jokes are rather clever. For example, have you heard the one about the older couple watching television one evening when the wife turned to the husband and said, "Dear, I'd like some ice cream. Would you go get us some?" He replied, "Of course, sweetheart, what kind would you like?" She said, "I want vanilla and get some chocolate syrup for topping. Oh, and you'd better write it down."

"Now, dear," he replied, "surely you don't think I need a list to buy just two items," and out the door he went. Thirty minutes later he returned and handed a sack to his wife. She looked inside, saw two cans of tomato soup, and announced angrily, "You old goat, you forgot the crackers!"

But joking aside, you probably want some hard data about what is going on in your mind—why your "forgetter" seems to work better with age? I know why; I learned it years ago . . . but I can't remember!

Our memory consists of three separate but related processes. (I'm not a psychologist or a memory expert, but I will try to explain these processes in lay language.) The first is *registration* (or impression). Registration happens when we have an experience and then consciously (or even unconsciously) place it in the storage area of our brain. The second process is called *retention*. This happens as we are able to hold on to some of the details of those past experiences that were stored away. The third process is *recall*, when we bring the details of those past experiences out of storage and into our consciousness. Now, can you remember the three Rs of memory?

When we find ourselves unable to remember something (an event, a person, a name, etc.), it means that one or more of these processes has failed—temporarily. I say *temporarily* because you are probably like my wife and me: you remember this afternoon what you forgot this morning.

The fact is that *all* people, young and old, forget things from time to time. I have no statistics (if indeed anyone has ever tried to compile the frequencies of our memory lapses), but it seems that when we are younger, we easily overlook such lapses. It is when we become older that we grow more concerned about our forgetfulness. All the while, of course, conventional wisdom asserts that we are supposed to become more forgetful as we age.

Short-term memory supposedly deteriorates first, while long-term memory deteriorates later. Casual observation appears to support this proposition. Haven't we all encountered a person who can (and does) describe in vivid detail an event that happened fifty years ago, yet has no clue that his daughter and grandchildren visited last week? Of course, in that regard, who is present to attest to the veracity of the person's recall of that event fifty years earlier?

Another aspect of psychological change has to do with learning. Conventional wisdom here is sheer nonsense! When people cite the old, rundown cliché "You can't teach an old dog new tricks," they do a terrible disservice to older people. Everybody knows that the cliché refers to humans, not dogs, but unfortunately not everyone knows it is untrue.

I said earlier that we are responsible for having accurate information. Thankfully, considerable research has tested and measured the learning ability of older adults. Here are the overwhelming results:

1. Changes in learning ability due to aging appear to be small. It is much more likely that impairment in learning is due to a prior incapacity or some debilitation in the individual.[1]

2. As a group, older adults are somewhat slower in learning new material than they were when they were younger and in comparison with younger cohorts.

3. Attitudes toward learning may change with age:
    a. Older individuals may be less ready to learn than when they were younger.
    b. Older persons may attempt to solve problems on the basis of what they already know rather than to learn new solutions.

Certainly these findings are inconsistent with the meaning of the cliché—that older individuals are *unable* to learn. Of course, the tragedy is that many members of our society believe the fallacy and perpetuate it by repeating it to anyone who will listen.

THE SOCIOLOGICAL DIMENSION

A third aspect of the aging process is the sociological, which has to do with human relationships. What does aging have to do with our associations and interactions with other people? As persons age, do they maintain social relationships as in their younger years, or do they withdraw? What does self-esteem have to do with our social relationships? How might retirement affect his/her social interactions?

During our young-adult and middle-adult years, we associate with an expanding number of people. Some of these relationships are job-related; others relate to our memberships in a variety of organizations. If we assess these relationships, we usually find that while we enjoy some of them, we merely tolerate others that seem to us expedient. Research shows that our relationships in later life generally mirror these earlier experiences.

At retirement, for example, we ordinarily terminate a number of social associations. If some of these job-related relationships have blossomed into true friendships, however, we may strive to retain them. Though we no longer spend time at work with our colleague-friends, we will make the effort to see them in other contexts.

The same logic holds true regarding the groups to which we belong. We decide to continue or discontinue memberships in civic or professional organizations largely based upon the significant social relationships established there through the years.

Social relationships are based upon personality factors as well as experiences. Some folks are more "people persons" than others. They seem to thrive on being with people, and in all likelihood, they will not wish to withdraw into themselves as they grow older. They will work to retain former relationships and seek to replace those that are lost through retirement or other social group termination.

On the other hand, some folks seem more satisfied and comfortable when they are alone. When retirement comes for them, they welcome the opportunity to pull away from colleagues. Chances are good that such folks will not seek to replace lost associations simply because those relationships are relatively unimportant to them. We need to understand that neither of these extremes is necessarily pathological; both are quite common.

As we grow older, we will do well to get in touch with our feelings concerning our relationships with other people. To the extent that these feelings are important to us, we will want to realistically maintain or discontinue our contact with others.

A word of warning may be appropriate here. Some of us in our senior years may find ourselves responsible for a person more senior than we (e.g., a parent). In such an instance, we should take care not to impose our personality whims relative to social relationships onto this other person. An illustration should help make this point: a man I know (I'll call him Timothy) is a responsible son and caregiver. His mother, Helen, is a recent widow. Three or four months after his father's death, Tim was visiting with Helen and their discussion centered on her daily activities and involvement outside her home. Tim thinks his mom is becoming reclusive, for she doesn't go outside her home very often. Helen is a music lover and has a large collection of classical recordings. She is content to spend most days listening to her music and putting together a family album containing memorabilia gathered over a forty-year period of time. Friends and other family members who drop by and call periodically feel that Helen is adjusting beautifully. She seems very happy despite times of melancholy when she shares remembrances of her late husband, Ed.

The problem is that Tim is a people person. His personality is outgoing and demonstrative, and, unfortunately, he feels that others—especially his mother—should be that way too. Without realizing it, he pressures Helen to get out more: have lunch at the county senior center, join a weekly bridge club, reactivate her membership and involvement in the local DAR chapter.

To be sure, Helen was more active as a younger woman, and both she and Ed were involved in community affairs. But now she is content to spend more time at home with her chosen activities. Her personality is, and always has been, more introverted than her son's.

What is my point? We all should recognize personality differences and honor them. We should not try to force our prescription for happiness onto others. If Helen were depressed, Tim and others would be aware. As a loving caregiver, Tim needs to appreciate his and Helen's differences and back off.

CONCLUSIONS

1. The aging process is real, inevitable, and irresistible. It is changing each of us one day at a time.

2. A significant component of aging takes place "between the ears." By this I mean that our attitudes are critically important. We can decide to look forward to growing older, or we can decide to dread it. If we convince ourselves that growing older will be dreadful, we can make it so. We can cause ourselves to become bitter, disgruntled old people. Thankfully, the reverse is also true. Our attitude is usually the deciding factor.

3. The human organism in all its aspects is tremendously resilient. Thus, we have great capacity to adapt to our aging changes. To do so successfully, we must have as much correct information as we can gather as we seek to develop and maintain a positive outlook on life.

QUESTIONS FOR DISCUSSION

1. We all have heard statements like the following and/or have made them ourselves.

> "July is almost over. Goodness! Where has this year gone?"
>
> "I'm going to be ___ years old next week. I can't believe it. Time is passing so quickly!"

Why do you think time seems to move more quickly as we grow older? How important is it to pause and remind ourselves that time is moving at exactly the same rate it always has?

2. What are the differences between your memory lapses and those of a person with severe dementia (e.g., of the Alzheimer's disease type)? Shouldn't knowing such distinctions eliminate unnecessary fears?

3. Are you an introvert or an extrovert (or do you know)? Do you feel that persons of any personality type can be useful in God's kingdom? Why?

4. What adjustments are you making to compensate for the aging changes that you are experiencing? Are you remembering to be joyful, rather than discouraged, as you make these adjustments?

Chapter Two
COLOR US BLUE

If ever an age group in the United States was justified in feeling sad and gloomy—blue—regarding its station in life, the elderly today are that group. Negativity associated with old people and with the aging process is rampant. This fact first became evident to me almost thirty years ago when I was completing the research for my dissertation. I was studying four different groups of respondents to a survey about aging: three groups consisted of young adults; the other was made up of older adults. All respondents reported negative feelings about the aged, but the group of older adults was the most negative of all. These attitudes represent a major reason for my writing this book, and they are the chief focus of this chapter.

A REVOLUTIONARY SHIFT

Our nation is about two-and-a-quarter centuries old. During the first hundred of these 226 years, the status of the elderly in society changed dramatically.

In colonial America, age was highly honored—much as it is today in other societies. The elderly were so highly respected that early census data suggested that some folks reported themselves to be older than they actually were. In fact, did you ever wonder why jurists in colonial times wore powdered wigs? It was to represent the wisdom of age that was thought to be needed in our courts of law.

During the next hundred years, however, a revolutionary transformation occurred: respect and reverence for the aged gave way to fear and disdain of the old. A "wise old man" became an "old geezer"; a "venerated old mother" was viewed as an "old fuddy-duddy." This negativism toward the old remains with us today. Why?

The following concepts, as they apply to our older population, will provide some of the answers. You may at once be surprised and alarmed as this discussion unfolds. I hope you will examine your own beliefs and feelings as we look at those of our overall population.

MYTHS

A myth is an old traditional story handed down through the ages to explain how something connected to man or nature came to be. Myths contain beliefs and opinions not based on fact or reality but based on casual observation. The problem with myths is that they do not serve us well in describing truth.

Cary Kart began his gerontology textbook with ten statements preceded with these instructions: "Read each item carefully, and indicate whether you believe it to be true or false."[1] Here are the ten statements:

___ *Senility* inevitably accompanies old age.

___ Most old people are *lonely and isolated* from their families.

___ The majority of old people are in *poor health*.

___ Old people are more likely than younger people to be *victimized by crime*.

___ The majority of old people live in *poverty*.

___ Old people tend to become *more religious* as they age.

___ Older workers are *less productive* than younger ones.

___ Old people who retire usually suffer a decline in health and *early death*.

___ Most old people have *no interest in, or capacity for, sexual relations*.

___ Most old people *end up in* nursing homes and other *long-term care institutions*.

Take a few moments to answer these items yourself. Later, I'll give you the correct answers; and if you are curious about how scientific research supports these answers, please turn to appendix A for a brief description.

Look again at the concepts found in these statements (I italicized them): senility, loneliness, poor health, victims of crime, poverty, less productivity, early death, no interest in sexual relations, destined for institutionalization. Is this what is in store for us when we become old? Do these concepts accurately describe old age in the United States?

Here is what Kart said: "If you answered 'false' to all 10 statements, you have a perfect score; 'true' responses indicate misconceptions about old people and the aging process."[2]

Are you surprised? Are you relieved? Just remember that these myths represent what most people in our society believe and feel about our elderly citizens.

STEREOTYPES

While the term *stereotype* probably originated in the printing industry to describe the casting of a mold to create an image or form, in our context it is a fixed idea or a popular conception regarding the looks, actions, and so forth, of a certain type of person. Stereotypes simplify and generalize reality. They may be either positive or negative, but in neither case do they adequately describe the "real thing."

Simplification, of course, makes it easier and more convenient for us to comprehend people and things around us. However, it minimizes the individual differences among members of certain groups, and it glosses over the wonderful diversity God has given to his creatures.

A positive stereotype of the elderly is this: "All old people are wise." What a nice thing to say, but what an inadequate thing to believe! A negative stereotype of the elderly is this: "All old people are childlike." What an irresponsible thing to say, and what an inadequate thing to believe!

Research has helped us learn how stereotypes of the aged have developed and how they are perpetuated. One way is through everyday aphorisms (short, concise statements expressing a general truth), which become clichés (expressions that become stale with excessive use). In the previous chapter I cited the well-known, oft-used cliché, "You can't teach an old dog new tricks." This negative belief and expression about older people is based on conventional wisdom, but it is inconsistent with scientific knowledge. Though many people think it's cute, in truth it is misleading and damaging. I wonder how many older people have heard it, believed it, internalized it, and given up trying to learn anything new in their old age. How very sad that is!

A second way in which stereotypes concerning the aged form is due to limited or nonexistent contact or experience with older persons. This can be explained in part by the fact that we are a society of nuclear families (i.e., one or two generations living in the same household—typically parents and their young children). This pattern, of course, is a change from the extended families of several generations ago, when members of three or more generations lived in the same household. A chief consequence of this change is that young children have minimal contact with their grandparents, so opinions are formed that are often fragmentary and generalized.

Myths and stereotypes are also communicated through the mass media. Many cartoonists, for example, have had great success depicting misleading notions (both positive and negative) about the elderly. They have done this to entertain, perhaps not knowing how their messages have been detrimental to the causes and prospects of our older citizens. Now and again, thoughtful depictions are presented; but typically the cartoons are insidiously damaging.

With the advent of television more than half a century ago, images of the elderly have become more direct and poignant. Studies of television programming have yielded these conclusions: the images of the elderly are generally negative, and the elderly are underrepresented in comparison with their numbers in the overall population.

While it is difficult to know how potentially damaging the effects of these findings might be, my point is that all messages that mislead, whether overtly or through innuendo, contribute to myths and stereotypes.

PREJUDICE

Social scientists and others who study attitudes—what they are and how they are measured—often specify three distinct components: (1) beliefs (cognitions), (2) feelings (affections), and (3) behavior (intended or real actions). To illustrate, consider this attitude mindset: (1) "I *believe* that old people have passed their usefulness in the business world" (cognition), (2) "I *do not like* working with old people" (feeling), (3) I *will not consider* this old person's resumé for our current job opening" (intended action). Both stereotypes and myths demonstrate the belief component along with a third—prejudice. Prejudice is an attitude or opinion formed before the facts are known; the concept derives from the term *prejudgment.*

Everyone is a victim of prejudices because no one can escape their far-reaching tentacles. Some of us already have been the objects of prejudicial beliefs. The fact of our individual and group differences makes us potential recipients. Some of us are classified as members of a so-called minority group; thus our potential victimization is increased exponentially. All of us, because we are aging and one day will be classified as being "old," are potential victims.

Less-obvious victims of prejudices are those of us who have been taught these prejudices from others who should know better. This learning took place during our young and formative years, when we were impressionable and vulnerable. We didn't know enough to question what we were being told about other "different" people, nor did it occur to us that members of our family and other significant adults would misrepresent the truth in their teachings. I personally was a victim of prejudiced teachings. Years later, when I began to question what I had been taught and had blindly accepted, I was not comforted to discover that my teachers had been victims of those who went before them.

The lesson to be learned here is twofold: first, many well-intentioned people teach lies because they never sought the truth about what they were being told; and secondly, when we discover untruths, they must be rectified immediately.

What recourse have victims of prejudice had in our society? The answer is, "Not much." Victims are often in powerless positions. What's more, we have learned that attitude changes are particularly difficult to effect; they cannot be legislated!

Young children, on the receiving end of prejudicial attitudes, have been taught a saying that we all have heard and probably used: "Sticks and stones may break my bones, but names will never hurt me." We usually interpret this to mean, "I don't care what you say about me, but don't take any action against me." My view is that being called pejorative names hurts, but discrimination hurts more.

DISCRIMINATION

Though the relationship between prejudice and discrimination is very real, it is not always neat and easy to understand. Attitude usually precedes, and even causes, behavior, but the reverse is occasionally true as well.

Discrimination generally means distinguishing between things that are different. In the context of our discussion, discrimination refers to the mistreatment of another person or group based on perceived differences of that person or group. In the last century, the terms *racism* (discrimination based on race) and *sexism* (discrimination based on sex or gender) were joined by *ageism,* a term first coined by Robert Butler to indicate "a process of stereotyping and discrimination against people because they are old."[3]

A classic example of ageism was the mandatory retirement laws existing in our society prior to 1967 (when the Age Discrimination in Employment Act began a process of rescinding those laws). Mandatory retirement was based on one or more of the following beliefs: (1) older workers are less productive, (2) older workers can't keep pace with younger workers, (3) older workers are unwilling to work for lower salaries.

Many battles have been fought in our streets, in our halls of learning, in our court rooms, and in Congress over issues related to prejudice and discrimination. Only in the past half century have we enacted legislation guaranteeing civil rights, equal rights in employment, and such, in an effort to address the adverse effects of discriminatory practices.

SUMMARY

It is our responsibility—individually and as a society—to gather correct information about the elderly and the aging process of change. To do this we must determine what is true and then perpetuate these truths, thereby eliminating untruths and half-truths.

Proper awareness of the aging process demands that we do this. What's more, successful adjustment to aging changes cannot be effected until we do so.

QUESTIONS FOR DISCUSSION

1. Do you hold prejudiced beliefs about any group(s) of people? Are they positive or negative? Are they based upon fact or error? Are you comfortable with these beliefs?

2. What do you think older people should do to address the overall negativity toward them as a group in

our society? What can you do as an individual? What can your church or denomination do collectively?

3. Did you initially realize that all ten of Kart's statements about the elderly were false? What does this say to you about your knowledge of the aging process and the aged in the United States?

4. Have you ever been victimized by prejudiced beliefs and their subsequent discrimination? What did you do? In retrospect, what should you have done?

Chapter Three

EXERCISE AND NUTRITION: AN UNBEATABLE COMBINATION

Did you think me somewhat audacious in chapter 1 when I suggested that

- growing older can be a process to be enjoyed, and
- old age can be a period of time to be relished?

Perhaps you were thinking, *Doesn't this guy know about debilitating illnesses, neglect, and abuse of older people as well as a host of other unfortunate situations we see and hear daily in the media?*

I do know about these things, but what I don't know is which, if any, of these will affect me—or you. Studies of aging as a process of change and of aging persons are often as statistical as they are descriptive. Conclusions provide information on what "happens" to the *typical* older person, and from these findings we may infer what is *atypical*. We can then project the possibilities that lie in wait for us individually.

Here is an illustration of what I mean. Studies reveal that about three-fourths of all elderly in the U.S. are living independently. This means that one-fourth are living in some degree of dependence. Which of these two groups typify the elderly? More importantly, in which of the two groups would you reasonably expect to be during your senior years? If you got the answers to both questions correct, you should be able to agree with my summary contention: I can choose to look forward to becoming a typical older person (as regards independence), or I can dread becoming an atypical older person. The choice is mine—and yours!

The fact that none of us knows what is in our future (except God's promise of eternal life for all who have accepted his Son as Savior) is the "stuff" of which faith is made. Of course, our genetic footprints are already set, and they may affect our quality of life. On the other hand, because of our freedom to make choices (human volition), we obviously do have some input as regards our future. We are responsible for what we do now, and the decisions we make will affect us later in life. Our quality of life in later years depends, in part, on what we do today.

We who have enjoyed a good measure of quality of life in our younger years will want to carry this into our later years. Most older persons today are enjoying a reasonably good quality of life (as shown by all the ways by which we measure it: happiness, satisfaction, living independently, etc.). Those who are now approaching senior adulthood have good reason to expect this as well. However, what we do now in terms of lifestyle, diet, exercise, work/rest habits, stress management, and so forth, may significantly affect quality of life later.

Consider the following contrast:

Ellen W. is in her late 50s, but friends say she looks and acts perhaps ten years younger. Ask her and she'll tell you how young she feels and that calendar years don't really count.

Betty M., on the other hand, is about the same age. However, she both looks and acts much older. If you ask her, she'll tell you how she worries about her health and about growing old.

Ellen and Betty are both 56, born only months apart. However, Ellen's "health age" is that of a woman only 48 years of age. In other words, her chance of dying in the next ten years is the same as that of a woman eight years younger. Betty's health age, on the other hand, is closer to a woman who is in her early 60s!

Why should two people of the same chronological age have health ages that are so far apart? There are many reasons, and heredity is

one of them. But how you take care of yourself—physically and emotionally—can substantially increase or decrease your health age.

And here's an important point: if you haven't
been taking care of yourself, you can still change
some of your ways and get back some of those
lost years. Yes, in a sense, you can *grow
younger*—not in chronological years, of course,
but in your health age.[1]

While the cliché cited in chapter 1—"You can't
teach an old dog new tricks"—is inaccurate regarding
the elderly, here is a better one: "An ounce of preven-
tion is worth a pound of cure." I'm convinced this philosophy (advice) is indeed true where one's health is
concerned, and our health is surely a chief factor in
quality of life.

Most diseases associated with old age are the
result of many years of poor health habits.
Heart disease, the number one cause of death,
often begins in early childhood. It takes many
years before it results in a heart attack that
causes death. Yet, no matter what our age, there
are actions we can take to begin reducing not
only the risk of a heart attack, but also other
hazards to our health. Good health habits can

help us to avoid or reduce the severity of numerous physical and mental diseases, ranging from cancer to psychological depression.[2]

For more than a generation our society has been beset with books, articles, plans, programs, self-help groups, and the like designed to develop our health consciousness. Most of these efforts have centered on nutrition (diet) and exercise. Thus, Americans have been counting calories and fat grams and attempting to establish and maintain a regular exercise program. Those who begin these efforts by consulting a physician and who remain faithful to their regimen will more than likely reap rewards later—a better quality of life and perhaps even extended years.

I have no *easy* solution to help people develop a health consciousness; I have only the resolve to emphasize the importance of good health habits. Here's why. Paul wrote to the church in Corinth: "Do you not know that *your bodies* are members of Christ himself? . . . [H]e who unites himself with the Lord is one with him in spirit. . . . Do you not know that *your body* is a temple of the Holy Spirit?" (1 Cor. 6:15a, 17, 19a, emphasis mine).

My purpose in the remainder of this chapter is not to make you feel bad. Instead it is simply to affirm what you should already know: What you do with yourself *now* will significantly influence what you will be like *later.* This is true in *all* dimensions of your life: physical, mental, social, and spiritual.

Being overweight, out of shape, and feeling less energetic than we might feel are not matters relating to eternal life. They are, however, matters relating to the abundant life Jesus desires for us (see John 10:10). I also believe that Paul's reference to our bodies as temples for God's Holy Spirit has relevance in our physical and psychological/emotional aspects. If you are overweight and/or out of shape and/or sluggish (non-energetic), and particularly if you are displeased with these conditions, I hope you will use these thoughts to consider bringing yourself into alignment with God's standards. Our good shape should be

- for God's glory,
- for our own edification, and
- a model for others.

NUTRITION

You have heard it said, "You are what you eat," and I say to you, "Indeed so!" Twice a year for several years running I had the dubious honor of stopping by our local meat market to pick up what my wife had ordered from the butcher: twenty-five pounds of fat that had been trimmed from his many cuts of meat. I brought this box of fat home so Deanna could take it to "show and tell" at the nutrition class she taught at our church. It was very graphic to note that twenty-five pounds of excess fat in our bodies looks very much like the contents of that box. Yuck!

She pointed out to her class that our excess fat, which results primarily from our food intake (type and amount) and eating habits, can be substantially reduced and essentially eliminated. Effecting such a change is never easy, and it requires considerable commitment and persistence. But those who do it experience a joyful life change; all who commit to lose the fat and are faithful to maintain a healthy weight are pleased with their success.

Unfortunately, there always are some who are not committed for the long haul. They experience dramatic weight loss but then are unwilling to sustain the new eating habits. Falling back into old habits, their weight begins to return, and most become discouraged—even depressed. Some become caught in a cycle of weight gains and losses—the "yo-yo effect," a series of ups and downs of body weight. This effect, according to some nutrition/health experts, may be even more stressful to the body than remaining at a plateau, albeit overweight.

EATING HABITS

Casual observation suggests that few people are aware of the importance of eating habits as they relate to body weight. Annette Natow and Jo-Ann Heslin have provided some suggestions on "how to eat"—suggestions that aim to change some lifelong patterns regarding food intake. To help you get in touch with healthy eating habits, please evaluate each of the following nine pairs of statements. Mark the one statement in each pair that you feel is the better eating habit. After you have completed the exercise, you may wish to review the authors' comments and recommendations in appendix B.

Eating Habits: Which Is Better for Me?

1. Eat only when you are hungry. ___
   Eat only at prescribed times. ___

2. Eat until you are pleasantly (not overly) full. ___
   Stop eating when you can still eat a little more. ___

3. When at home, vary your place of eating. ___
   When at home, eat at one place only. ___

4. Eat quickly, but do not gulp your food. The slower you eat, the more you will tend to eat. ___
   Eat as slowly as you can. Chew slowly and think about how the food tastes. ___

5. Don't read or watch television while eating. ___
   Watching television and, to a lesser extent, reading will help you be distracted from your hunger. ___

6. Use a smaller plate (salad or luncheon size); usual portions of food will appear generous. ___
   Always use a dinner plate; slightly fuller portions will negate a perceived need to return for second helpings. ___

7. Keep snack foods throughout the house to help
   take the edge off a voracious appetite. ___
   Don't leave snack food throughout the house.
   Keep all foods out of sight when you are not
   eating. ___
8. Always clean your plate; this will help you not
   wish to have second portions. ___
   Practice leaving a little food on your plate. You
   really don't have to eat it all. ___
9. Always eat three meals a day. Missing a meal to
   "splurge" later is unwise. ___
   It is OK to "splurge" occasionally, and you
   should skip a meal to accommodate such an
   intention. ___

EXERCISE

Movement is life! Exercise is maintenance! Interesting
thoughts, aren't they? They could be liberating thoughts
as well if you are out of shape, if you have an untoned
body, and/or if your energy level is low. The following
quotation from Barbara Deane is revealing:

> Aging bodies, like aging buildings, need more
> maintenance as they grow older. . . . Gradually,
> our body metabolism slows down—on the aver-
> age of 5 percent per decade. This doesn't sound
> like much, but the woman who used to need
> 2,200 calories to maintain her body weight now

needs only 1,600. Unless she increases her activity or reduces her food intake, the excess will be stored as fat.[3]

HEALTHFUL BENEFITS

Exercise becomes increasingly important as we get older. Done regularly, exercise can improve our cardiovascular endurance, muscle strength, and flexibility. Let's consider each of these elements separately.

1. *Cardiovascular endurance.* This is the most vital element of fitness. It enables us to carry on activity for an extended period of time. To build such strength, we must enhance the cardiovascular system's ability to deliver oxygen and carry away cellular waste. Regular aerobic (with air) exercises increases the heart's capacity to pump more blood and thus deliver more oxygen to the cells of our body with greater efficiency.

The American College of Sports Medicine recommends aerobic-exercise sessions of fifteen to sixty minutes per day, three to five days per week. The following exercises are excellent: running, brisk walking, swimming, cycling, rowing, cross-country skiing, and rope skipping.

When regularly performed, such exercises reduce the risk of heart disease, help keep blood pressure at normal levels, and aid in weight control. Personally, I have found that exercising makes me feel more energetic and helps me handle stress better. It is exciting to try it and find that it works!

2. *Muscle strength.* Few older people wish to be power lifters, but all of us should be able to perform basic tasks. We need muscle strength to climb stairs, rise from a chair, lift grocery bags, push a vacuum cleaner, and wash a car. Well-toned muscles also help us maintain good posture and prevent injuries. Muscle strength also reduces the risk of osteoporosis because it protects against bone loss by increasing bone density.

You can build muscle strength and endurance through a process called "progressive resistance training." Resistance devices, such as weights, are applied to normal body motion. In a typical weight-training program, you lift or move weights in sets of repetitions, and the muscles develop. By varying muscle groups each day, none need ever be overextended.

3. *Flexibility.* This refers to the ability of the joints to move through their full range of motion. Good flexibility is thought to protect against muscle pulls and tears, to alleviate lower back pain, and to prevent muscle cramps. To improve flexibility, do slow, static stretches until a pulling (not painful) sensation is felt. These stretches should be held for ten seconds. Relax; then repeat. Over a period of days or weeks, work up to twenty and then thirty seconds per stretch. Stretching should be gradual and relaxed, with no bouncing.

GETTING STARTED ON AN EXERCISE PROGRAM

1. Before beginning, get a physician's approval.
2. Begin your program slowly and make increases gradually (an exercise physiologist can help with specifics).
3. For your workout:

    A. Warm up first—about five to ten minutes—to raise body temperature.

    B. Stretch.

    C. Work out.

    D. Cool down gradually.

    E. Enjoy a wonderful day!

4. Plan to continue exercising indefinitely.

If you have lapsed into a sedentary lifestyle (not necessitated by a debilitating illness) and if you will commit to changing those habits, you will be truly amazed at the exciting changes in store for you.

FINAL CONSIDERATIONS

If God is impressing upon you a need and a desire (you really need both) to make a change regarding your physical well-being, consider these final suggestions. First, invite another person to work with you. Your spouse could be an excellent choice if she/he is willing to assist and encourage you. A friend, whose goals are similar to yours, could also be a good choice. In lieu of an individual, a group of like-minded individuals might work well with you. On the other hand, working out with nonbelievers could provide opportunities to cultivate friendships and sow gospel seeds as well. Mutual encouragers breed long-lasting success.

Second, you need to know that dieting and exercising are complementary—they work best in combination. Attempting either without the other will require more time and bring less-favorable results.

Finally, realize that your goal must be for lifelong change. Halfhearted hit-and-miss attempts are unbecoming to children of God, and they will add to your frustration and displeasure. Eating improperly (excessively, nonnutritiously) is like other addictive behaviors—it can never be resumed without leading you back to where you started. Instead of being discouraged by this truth, trust God to help you make the necessary changes that will enable you to maintain your new, improved lifestyle.

You will be more joyful (live more abundantly) when you commit to give your best to live up to the lofty standards of the Lord in every aspect of your life. Though your goals may seem daunting at times, achieving them is possible—not in your perfection, but in God's power.

QUESTIONS FOR DISCUSSION

1. How do you personally feel about your "health age," as contrasted in the lives of Ellen W. and Betty M.? What do you think about the important point made in their stories: "If you haven't been taking care of yourself, you can still change some of your ways"?

2. When you think of your body as God's temple, how pleased are you with your treatment of that temple?

3. What are your thoughts and reaction to this statement: "Our good shape should be (1) for God's glory, (2) for our own edification, (3) a model for others"?

Chapter Four

DEPENDENCE—
INDEPENDENCE—
DEPENDENCE

In late 2001, one month past her 107th birthday, my great-aunt passed away. Born in 1894, Aunt Frances lived during the nineteenth, twentieth, and twenty-first centuries. She was quite a lady—remarkable really! As a young adult, she taught school in central Texas. As a young wife, she followed her husband around the oil fields in West Texas. During the war years, she was alone while Uncle Edgar served with the Merchant Marines.

Because they had no children, Aunt Frances was again left alone on their farm in Michigan when Uncle Edgar died thirty-five years ago. Thankfully, he had family members who took her "under their wings." As she slowly became dependent, she moved from the farm to a series of facilities designed to provide the care she needed.

While our society has a growing number of centenarians, very few live to the age of 107, and fewer still live in a dependent status as long as Aunt Frances did. Over a twenty-five-year period, she lived in four different types of care facilities, ranging from independent living to a skilled nursing home. While most of us are somewhat familiar with such facilities, few are aware that about three-fourths of our nation's senior adults actually live independently of such residences. Probably the most surprising fact is that only 5 percent of our elderly reside in nursing homes—a figure that has held steady for many years.

There are many players in these dependence-independence-dependence scenarios, but for our discussion we will focus on three: the older, dependent person; the caregiver; and caregiving programs and facilities.

THE DEPENDENT, OLDER PERSON

For some, dependency comes quickly: a stroke, a fall with ensuing debilities, an accident with long-term injuries, and so forth. For most, however, dependency encroaches insidiously—at first unnoticed, then suspected, and finally acknowledged. Nor are these changes just physical. An adult child, for example, might be asked, "What do you think of _____?", a question the parent has never asked before. Weeks or months later, that parent might ask, "What do you think I should do about this notice from my company regarding hospitalization options?" Still later, a similar need may be expressed this way: "Will you help me decide _____?" All of these questions are requests for help—increasingly explicit, even urgent; and the sensitive child should begin tuning in and listening/observing closely.

As changes continue to modify the aging individual, he or she realizes something new and, often, alarming: "I can no longer adapt successfully; I need help!" While some may readily request help, others may not yet be ready to admit what is happening. They will insist:

- "I can still drive."
- "I can still pay my bills and balance my checkbook."
- "I can still travel across the country to visit family as I've always done."

Denial may persist, but the time will come when a crisis brings full realization of their needs.

Sociologists and gerontologists use several terms to help explain these phenomena of change. *Role transitions* describes the changes from one role to another (e.g., middle adulthood to older adulthood). *Anticipatory socialization* describes the learning of a new role in preparation to taking on that new role. Unfortunately, in our culture the status of older adulthood is thought to be *roleless* (invisible or uncertain), or as Cary Kart puts it, "Whereas there is much prescribed activity associated with other life transitions, there is little prescribed activity that attends to old age."[1] So, in regards to change, the question is begged: "How do longtime independent adults know how to behave dependently?"

Here, then, is the essence of the struggle: unforeseen change, alarm (even panic), denial, uncertainty, fear, and seemingly no place to turn and no comfortable person to whom to turn. This progression may be followed by the "What if" syndrome:

- "What if I have to give up my house (or car, etc.)?"
- "What if I have to go to a nursing home?"
- "What if I lose my privacy?"

Enter . . .

THE CAREGIVER

A caregiver is that person who agrees—usually voluntarily, though sometimes for remuneration—to become responsible for one who has become dependent.

The typical caregiver is an adult female, usually a spouse but sometimes a daughter. Even a nonfamily member caregiver is usually female. In general, females are better nurturers, more intuitive, and generally better suited for the role. Even so, some males take on the role and do an excellent job.

Within the Christian community, the rationale for the spirit of caregiving is found in God's Fifth

Commandment: "Honor your father and your mother, so that you may live long in the land the LORD your God is giving you" (Exod. 20:12). Its reiteration in Deuteronomy 5:16 is essentially the same.

The wisdom of God is that his plan calls for family members to look after one another. Parents care for their dependent young; then in turn, adult children care for their dependent parents. Moses reminded the Israelites (and us): "Observe the LORD's commands and decrees that I am giving you today *for your own good*" (Deut. 10:13, emphasis mine). So, mark it down: The best, most successful, and God-honoring caregiving will come from the spirit (intention) of his Fifth Commandment!

The caregiver's task is not easy, so good preparation is vital. Please consider the following suggestions:

1. *Awareness.* Realize that your parent(s) may one day become dependent; therefore, decide *before that time* if you are willing to become their caregiver. If you are unwilling, ask yourself this question: "With whom will I want to entrust my parents' care?" When you determine an answer, discuss the eventuality with that person and arrive at a satisfactory agreement.

2. *Devise a plan.* When dependence reaches the point where action is necessary, bring together all principle players for a strategy session to develop a plan. I advise that the dependent person(s) be included if possible— you will encounter less opposition from those who

continue to have some voice in decisions impacting their future. A significant part of your plan will revolve around finding satisfactory solutions for the Activities of Daily Living (ADLs), basic self-care activities. These include bathing, dressing, toileting, getting into or out of a bed or chair, walking, getting outside the house or apartment, and feeding.

3. *Sibling unity.* If dependent parents have more than one child, God's commandment to "honor father and mother" applies to each child. Ideally, all the children will want to be involved in the care plan; however, geographical constraints and other restrictions may render equality of caregiving next to impossible. Nevertheless, a family plan that aims for sibling unity—meaning, agreement by all involved—will serve everyone in the best way. Such can be effected by lots of love, good communication, gathering appropriate and reliable information, taking time to thoroughly investigate all options, and lots of love. A family cannot take care of Mom and Dad well while bickering among themselves!

4. *Recognize both real and potential feelings.* A caregiver's feelings may run a wide gamut: pity, insensitivity, oversensitivity, frustration, anger, indifference, and such. These need to be acknowledged and addressed. Remember, too, that your dependent patient is also struggling with a new role and may be experiencing some of the same feelings. The apostle James's counsel is helpful here:

"Whenever you face trials of many kinds . . . [*persevere*].
. . . If any of you lacks *wisdom*, he should ask God, who
gives generously to all" (James 1:2b, 3, 5a, emphasis mine).

5. *Recognize role reversal.* This is another term used
by gerontologists. A classic example of role reversal is
when an aging parent and his/her adult child reverse their
roles. The phenomenon is very traumatic—particularly
when unanticipated. Several years ago Bob Carroll, a
physician friend of mine, experienced this very problem.
He was caring for his father, a victim of Alzheimer's. The
elder Mr. Carroll, an avid walker, was in the middle
stages of the disease. Because he had gotten lost several
times while walking in the neighborhood, he was now
content to simply walk around the yard of Bob's house.

Late one winter afternoon, it was misting rain and
about forty degrees. Bob drove into his driveway and
found his dad—dressed only in his shirtsleeves and
wearing no hat—walking around the house. Bob tells
the rest of the story this way: "I jumped out of my car,
ran over to my dad, and yelled, 'Get into the house right
now!' Dad meekly went into the house, and I returned
to my car feeling just awful. I cannot describe the
remorse I felt, for I had never before spoken to my dad
that way, in that tone of voice. I yelled at him as I might
yell at a child."

Because of the dementia accompanying Alzheimer's
disease, Mr. Carroll had become as a child, and Bob, of

necessity in the caregiver's role, had become as his father's parent.

Role reversal is seldom 100 percent (nor should it ever be), but it is wise to recognize the possibility that these kinds of changes may occur. The experience for Bob was worse because he was caught unaware.

CAREGIVING PROGRAMS AND FACILITIES

Accompanying the increase of dependent senior adults in the U.S.—in both numbers and percentage of population—is a proliferation of agencies offering one or more types of care. For some, these are last resorts on the continuum of care; for others, they are reasonable alternatives for families who—for various reasons—are unable to provide necessary care.

Sooner or later, every dependent older person and every caregiver will have to address the relative merits of care agencies. The following discussion provides a modicum of information about available options as well as some questions to consider concerning the pros and cons of institutionalization.

CONTINUING CARE AT HOME

Keeping one's parents in their own home seems to be the preference of most families. As dependency sets in, a caregiving plan might begin with home health care and/or adult day care.

Home Health Care. Using multidisciplinary services—skilled nursing, mental health care, financial and/or legal assistance, household management assistance, and such—home health care "aids the elderly person in the performance of activities of daily living."[2]

Costs are related to the services provided, so carefully examine your insurance to determine what services are covered. Most long-term care policies provide for home health services.

Adult Day Care. Technically speaking, this term applies to any service provided during the day, whether at home or elsewhere. The beauty of these services is that they are tailor-made for the individual's needs. Included within this category of care are social and health centers, day hospitals, strictly-social centers, and others.

Two especially noteworthy advantages of this option are: (1) length of hospitalization may be shortened if patients can have their needs met in day-care centers; and (2) caregivers may receive respite (relief) during the time their clients are in day care.

CONTINUOUS CARE RETIREMENT COMMUNITIES (CCRCs)

These multipurpose, multilevel care centers are groupings of residences designed for older adults whose needs (real and perceived) extend beyond what is provided by a private dwelling for which the older person is responsible. Typical CCRCs begin their range of services with dwellings (apartments, condominiums, bungalows, etc.) for *independent* older adults. Why is this, you may ask? It is to meet a growing demand of elderly persons who wish to relinquish responsibilities necessary for maintaining their own domicile.

These centers usually guarantee continuing care as it may be needed for the duration of the resident's life. Most CCRCs have up to four levels of care available:

1. *Independent living.* Residents at this level attend to their own basic needs (including all activities of daily living), and they have freedom to come and go as they please. Typical household chores such as changing light bulbs, unstopping a commode or sink, mowing the lawn, weeding the flower bed, and so on, are the center's responsibility. Such freedom does not come cheaply, but increasing numbers are opting for this arrangement.

2. *Assisted-living.* Living separately from those in the independent residences are those who must have some, or all, of their daily needs provided by others. These apartments are staffed by caregivers who provide needed assistance for the activities of daily living.

3. A step beyond assisted-living is *intermediate nursing care.* The distinctions at this level are usually made on the bases of type and amount of care prescribed by the patient's physician.

4. *Skilled nursing care.* The needs at this level call for specially qualified staff and equipment. High-level nurs-

ing skills and rehabilitative services are required, again as directed by the patient's physician.

While individual residents and family caregivers may make choices for levels 1 and 2, medical practitioners will determine care needs at levels 3 and 4.

When it becomes evident that the aging person's needs can no longer be satisfactorily met at home, preparation should begin immediately for other arrangements to be made. The following considerations may help make the decision-making process most effective:

1. Pray—asking for God's sovereign will to be revealed.
2. Patient(s), caregiver(s), and family should *together* discuss potential options.
3. These same players should visit potential care centers and ask pertinent questions.
4. Physician's diagnoses, prognoses, and suggestions concerning the patient should be considered.
5. When all appropriate data have been gathered, the principle players should develop a plan of action (with feasible contingencies).
6. A spokesperson should be selected to work directly with the CCRC and staff, and this spokesperson should be continually encouraged in her/his decisions.
7. The plan of action should be reviewed periodically for effectiveness.

8. Don't "look back" (Remember Lot's wife?), and don't second-guess one another.
9. Pray—for God's wisdom and guidance.

FINAL NOTE

Perhaps you are experiencing adult dependency for the first time, or you find yourself in the role of caregiver. You would do well to keep a record of your thoughts and experiences. I recommend a written journal. (Remember: your "forgetter" will be improving with age, so you probably will not want to keep just a "mental" record.)

Family members and friends who are one, even two, generations behind are watching you as a role model. From you they are learning what to expect from a dependent adult or from one who has accepted the responsibility of caring for someone who has become dependent. Who knows? One of them may one day be *your* caregiver. How helpful it would be for them to follow in the footsteps of someone with a loving, caring spirit. Your work and demeanor could be a wonderful example of edifying another.

QUESTIONS FOR DISCUSSION

1. Many adults dread the thought of becoming dependent—again. But if we live long enough, it will

happen. Which of the following scenarios would best serve you and your family?

A. I will fight dependency as long as I can and never consent to being institutionalized!

B. I will try to help my family make the best decision in my behalf, and I will try to adapt to the change as cheerfully as possible.

C. I will be passive about becoming dependent. Let someone else decide for me what I should do. I may not like it, but what can I do?

2. Have you ever found yourself in a parent-child role reversal? If so, reflect on your experience. In retrospect, how would you have done things differently? If you have never been involved in a role reversal, what might help you prepare for such a possibility?

3. Do you agree with the contention that old adulthood is a roleless role? What are some ways in which you can prepare for old age? What are some things you can teach younger persons to help them prepare for old age?

Chapter Five

HOW CAN YOU NOT TAKE IT WITH YOU?

When I spoke of the merits of independence in the previous chapter, it was to show the perils of having to revert to a dependent status. If we look more deeply into these realities, we find some other truths. Two of these truths should help you better understand what I wish to convey in this chapter: individual estate planning.

The first truth is this: All humans are really more dependent than they care to admit. The following illustrations will help verify this truth.

Humans are social animals; we constantly interact with one another. As we establish meaningful and enduring relationships, most of us allow ourselves to become vulnerable to others. Vulnerability means dependence, not independence.

When John Donne wrote three centuries ago that "no man is an island," surely he was calling to our attention the fact that humans are not created, nor do they exist, in a vacuum. In his famous "looking-glass self" concept, Charles Horton Cooley affirmed that we care about what we believe others think of us. Because of this, we are admitting a measure of dependency.

We use other persons as our sounding boards. We find it helpful, even essential, to bounce our ideas, opinions, hurts, questions, and such, off others who are significant to us. Here, as with the other examples, we are perpetuating some dependency.

The other truth that is relevant here is this: Independence carries with it some inherent dangers. Independence calls for self-sufficiency; both are valuable, but only to a point. When independence and self-sufficiency work across time to bring us success, we may conclude: "I have it made!" However, such an assertion can cause us to fall prey to the following temptations:

1. *Thinking too highly of ourselves.* Writing to the Romans, Paul put it this way: "For by the grace given me I say to every one of you: Do not think of yourself more highly than you ought, but rather think of yourself with sober judgment, in accordance with the measure of faith God has given you" (Rom. 12:3). When we leave God out of our success, we tread on thin ice!

2. *Boasting about the future.* James wrote this to the early Christians: "Now listen, you who say, 'Today or tomorrow we will go to this or that city, spend a year there, carry on business and make money.' Why, you do

not even know what will happen tomorrow. What is your life? You are a mist that appears for a little while and then vanishes. Instead, you ought to say, 'If it is the Lord's will, we will live and do this or that.' As it is, you boast and brag. All such boasting is evil" (James 4:13–16). Control of the future belongs to God, not to us.

3. *Overconcern with* our *possessions.* When Jesus was teaching a crowd of thousands, he told the parable of the rich fool:

> The ground of a certain rich man produced a good crop. He thought to himself, "What shall I do? I have no place to store my crops." Then he said, "This is what I'll do. I will tear down my barns and build bigger ones, and there I will store all my grain and my goods. And I'll say to myself, 'You have plenty of good things laid up for many years. Take life easy; eat drink and be merry.'" But God said to him, "You fool! This very night your life will be demanded from you. *Then who will get what you have prepared for yourself?*" This is how it will be with anyone who stores up things for himself but is not rich toward God. (Luke 12:16–21, emphasis mine)

The Lord is asking us, "Of what use will your amassed fortune (small or large) be to you when you die?"

Life expectancy tables reflect "the expected age at death of the average individual, granting current mortality rates from disease and accidents."[1] When I was born in 1937, my life expectancy was 59.3 years, but now that I have lived to age 65, my life expectancy is almost 80 years. While such statistics are important to the life insurance industry, they are much less important to me. What is important to me is the fact that I am a temporal, finite being with a spiritual dimension that is eternal. Possessions in this life will have no lasting value for me, for none will accompany my spirit into eternity with God. This is surely why the Lord Jesus told us to treasure up things incorruptible (heavenly things), because our treasures are in our hearts (Matt. 6:19–21).

Those of us who survive to old age (if indeed we know when old age begins), who understand God's plan, and who embrace Jesus as Lord and Savior surely begin to realize the fleeting nature of time and the relative unimportance of human possessions. While we all have experienced God's abundance, its manifestation and measurement differ from person to person. The real key to abundance is not what we have but who we are—in Christ. And who we are in Christ is what we will take with us into his eternity.

Having put our material possessions into their proper perspective (we possess them; they do not possess us), let's realize that God has chosen to give us whatever he has chosen to give us, and he expects us to be good stewards of those things. If we are doing this, then we should now begin arranging to dispense our estate in a responsible and effective manner. By responsible and effective I mean for the good of those to whom it is left.

A line from the song "Find Us Faithful" goes like this: ". . . and may all who come behind us find us faithful." We have a responsibility to those who are following us, just as we found in the previous chapter that we have a responsibility to some of those preceding us. We are to teach, train, and set an example for all who look to us to do these things. This responsibility also includes making provisions for leaving behind what we cannot take with us.

The suggestions that follow are for your consideration. As they apply to you, I recommend that you consult with your financial adviser and/or attorney for further clarification and action.

ASSET INVENTORY

As you begin to get your affairs in order, prepare a list of your assets, and find a safe place in which to keep the list.[2] Your list should be as exhaustive (complete) as you can make it and conducive to periodic reviews and updates. It also should include the location of original (and copies) of all documents associated with an asset.

To help you get started, consider the inclusion of the following items as they may apply to your estate:

- Income tax returns (with supporting data)
- Bank accounts (checking, savings, etc.)
- Business interests
- Deeds to properties
- Insurance policies (life, home, automobile, hospitalization, dental, long-term care, etc.)
- Wills (codicils)
- Trusts
- Pension plans (private, government, military, etc.)
- Savings-and-loan accounts
- Social Security records (estimation of benefits, etc.)
- Stocks, bonds, other securities
- Mortgage papers
- Military discharge records (DD 214)
- Survivor benefits programs
- List of credit cards (where to call if lost)
- Equipment and appliance records (model, serial numbers, maintenance agreements)
- Automobile titles and registrations (license receipts, maintenance agreements)
- Appraisals of valuable items (jewelry, furs, artwork, antiques, etc.)
- Educational records (diplomas, transcripts, certifications, etc.)
- Medical and immunization records

- Personal resumés
- Birth certificates (copies)
- Passports
- Other legal documents (powers-of-attorney, directives-to-physicians for health care, etc.)
- Marriage, divorce, adoption records
- Naturalization papers
- Savings bonds, certificates of deposit, money-market accounts
- Photographs of entire contents of home (room-by-room)

The list of your asset documents (not necessarily the documents themselves) should be located in a safe place. Many people opt for a safe-deposit box in their local bank. Should this be your choice, you will want to determine the following:

1. Who shall have access to the box? These individuals will need to be on the bank's authorization card and have a key for gaining access. If you and your spouse have joint access, be sure to ask about state law requirements in the event of your or your spouse's death.

2. Will access to the box during normal banking hours be adequate for all possible contingencies? If you envision a possible need for access during other than banking hours, you may want to consider another safe place.

A lockable, fireproof box in your home is another option. My wife and I have two of these, and we trust their security features. Not only do we have our list of assets, we also keep some of our documents in the boxes. The main advantage is quick and sure access at anytime.

Unsafe places that have been used by people in the past (hopefully no longer) are: (1) between the mattress and the box springs on their bed, (2) in a can buried in the backyard (X marks the spot!), (3) in the deep freezer (good for "cold" cash!), and (4) in a cardboard box in the attic or in the back of a closet.

One other question is important: Who else needs a list of your assets and/or copies of any of the documents listed? Possible answers to this question are:

1. Your attorney—legal documents
2. Your children—legal documents
3. The executor/executrix of your will—wills, trusts
4. The trustee of your trust—wills, trusts
5. Your physician—directive to physician for health care
6. Your tax accountant—tax records, etc.
7. Other? _____.

WILLS AND TRUSTS

The most foolish of all mistakes regarding one's estate is to die intestate (without a will). "If you die intestate, state law will govern how your estate is distributed—regardless of your wishes and the situation with your dependents. If you wish to control what happens to your estate, you must have a will and it must be valid under the law of your particular state."[3]

In my opinion, all adults should have a will, and it should be updated periodically to reflect current wishes. Since few married couples die together, each should have a current will.

"A trust is a legal device under which a person gives certain of his/her property to a trustee who will manage it for the benefit of one or more beneficiaries."[4] There are several different types of trusts, so consultation with an attorney will help determine exactly what is needed for what you intend. Whether or not you have a trust, you need a will.

DURABLE POWER OF ATTORNEY

With this legal document, an individual may designate and authorize another to act in his/her behalf with regard to property and financial matters. The adjective *durable* means that the arrangement continues even when the person who gives the power is incapacitated.

Several years ago, my father-in-law suffered a stroke that rendered him aphasic and mentally incapable of decision making. He never recovered these faculties before he died some eighteen months later. During this time, my mother-in-law needed to make some decisions about several pieces of rental property with deeds recorded in her husband's name alone. Unfortunately she had no power of attorney to act in his behalf. In their state it was necessary to have him publicly declared mentally incompetent. This included a visit from the local sheriff and a notice of the declaration published in the newspaper. My mother-in-law suffered a good deal of mental anguish needlessly, simply because she and her husband failed to address this need beforehand.

You should also consider having a durable power of attorney *for health care decisions*. This specifically allows a designated health care surrogate to interpret your living will (i.e., directives for withholding life-sustaining procedures in the event of certain stated contingencies).

GIFTING—NOW OR LATER?

A recent discussion with two friends brings to mind one other issue that could be very important to many folks.

Tax laws today allow for tax-free gifting of ten thousand dollars per year, per person to family members. This means that a married couple could give each of their children twenty thousand dollars per year tax free. Because of estate (death) taxes, some parents are electing to do this, but several important questions should be raised:

1. Is it your or your children's money?
2. What are your reasons for giving it *now* rather than *later*?
3. Do they *need* it now rather than later?
4. Can they handle it better now rather than later?
5. If you give it now, will you *enable* their dependency upon you?
6. Do you realize that your children are different from one another and, consequently, the answers to the above questions may be different for each child?
7. Laws for estate taxes are changing (liberalizing), and some believe they may be rescinded in the near future. Do you know how to stay current on these laws?

Some children would profit immensely from gifting, but others would be hurt in the long run (like the prodigal son described in Luke 15). We, as prospective givers, are responsible for making this determination. We need to be fair, but we also must be wise.

SUMMARY

If God has given you an estate, be it modest or substantial, and you realize that you cannot take it with you when you die, how can you leave it in a God-pleasing, responsible way? It is never too soon to answer this question and make the necessary arrangements.

QUESTIONS FOR DISCUSSION

1. During all the years of your life with your children, what do you "owe" them? Which of the following apply for you?

A. Love and nurture

B. A godly example of living

C. An education

D. An inheritance

E. Substantial gifts along the way

F. Unconditional love

G. A memorable upbringing

H. Your time (quantity and quality)

2. What is your opinion of the bumper sticker you probably have seen on many vehicles: "I'm spending my kids' inheritance!"?

3. Is it really feasible for you to consider compiling a list of your assets? If you should make the effort to do this, how will it help you deal with your estate and prepare for your retirement?

Chapter Six
O-H (B-P) S

That morning, October 4, 1995, began as most of my Wednesday mornings. I was working out at Ultrafit, my exercise club, having begun just after six o'clock. After thirty minutes of aerobic exercises, I began to feel a heaviness in the center of my chest. Though not a severe pain, it was uncomfortable—and lasting. After spending ten or fifteen minutes hoping it would go away (I wanted it to be a muscle spasm or some other innocuous possibility), I asked for help. An ambulance was called, and I was taken to the hospital emergency room.

Within an hour after the chest pain began, it was gone and has never returned. However, the concerns and the questions were not gone. That afternoon I underwent a heart catheterization. The angiogram revealed a blockage in my left anterior descending (LAD) artery. The cardiologist estimated a 90 percent blockage of the blood flow. What was I to do?

To do nothing was not an option! How about angioplasty or the installation of a stint to open the plaque-blocked artery? Yes, it might work; it might work indefinitely. On the other hand, it might work only temporarily.

"It depends," said the doctor.

"On what," I asked.

"We don't know for sure," said he. "The success rate through the years for these procedures has been good, but we are concerned that the LAD is rather long and narrow. It is not the best candidate for angioplasty and stints."

"What is another option?" I asked.

"We can bypass the LAD and most likely use your left mammary artery. This procedure should provide better results and be more permanent, and we won't have to use a vein from your leg. We believe this to be the better long-range solution."

With little hesitation, my wife and I opted for the single bypass surgery. It was completed two days later, and five days after that I was home from the hospital. The day after that, exactly one week from the initial chest pains, I attended choir practice, but I must admit I couldn't sing too well.

Why do I include my experiences with <u>o</u>pen-<u>h</u>eart (<u>by</u>pass) <u>s</u>urgery? (You will note that the underlined letters represent the cryptic title of this chapter.) There are several reasons. The first is that this surgery is becoming increasingly common—even routine—with greater successes and lasting benefits. More importantly, I think, is the fact that it represents one of a multitude of experiences we possibly will face as we grow older. Please note, also, that it exemplifies a malady over which we have relatively little control. Let me explain why I believe this to be true and why it is important to us.

In chapter 1, I wrote of having a good weight-height ratio. This has been effected by a combination of regimens as regards both diet and exercise (chap. 3). In short, I have been in good physical condition throughout my adult years. As you can imagine, many friends and family members were surprised (even shocked) when they heard of my chest pains and ensuing surgery. Admittedly, I was surprised as well, for I had hoped that my lifestyle might somehow preclude any cardiovascular anomalies.

As the doctors analyzed my situation, they concluded that my genetic background was the major culprit. My maternal grandfather succumbed to heart disease at age sixty-five. My father had a heart attack when he was fifty-eight and bypass surgery when he was seventy-six. Dad died last year, at age eighty-six, of complications associated with congestive heart failure. Even so, no one has told me with assurance what combination of factors led to my cardiovascular problem. Therefore, how can I possibly know whether I could have done anything to either forestall or prevent this experience? The best plan for me is to take my Lord's advice about worry (see Matt. 6:25–34), fix what is wrong, and get on with living in trust and commitment to the Lord.

One other observation may be helpful: as best we can tell, my rapid recovery from major invasive surgery was due primarily to good physical conditioning. All of my health caregivers were complimentary as to the quick progress I made. Probably the best indicator of this was the instruction given me by my thoracic surgeon when he released me from the hospital. He said, in effect:

- Don't drive or lift anything weighing more than ten pounds for the next six weeks.
- Return to your exercise program as soon as you feel like it.
- Eat what you have been eating.
- Return to your work as soon as you feel like it.
- I don't need to see you again. Go to your family doctor.

Consider the importance of attitude in all of this. Most of my loved ones, friends, and colleagues, though initially surprised at my problem, rejoiced with me at how things worked out. Only one colleague said, in effect, "If this has happened to Dave, why should I be concerned with eating in a healthy manner? Bring on the doughnuts [junk food]!" Thankfully, he was not serious, but someone else could be. Our perspective in all matters is extremely important!

I'd like to make a final point. From the beginning of my chest pains and the immediate response aftermath, I do not recall feeling panic, depression, or fear. Without question, God was with Deanna and me throughout the ordeal. We felt secure with him from the beginning . . .

1. in the decision of *what* to do. I remember only a moment of uncertainty in deciding to have surgery. While the lesser-certain, outpatient procedures were appealing, the longer-term "fix" seemed the wiser choice.

2. in the decision of *where* to have the surgery. Several others in our church who had had similar problems advised me to go to Houston, Dallas, or Tyler (all within easy reach of our home in Nacogdoches, Texas), locations with more heart specialists and more reputable facilities. My cardiologist recommended a relatively-new-to-our-area thoracic surgeon, and after meeting with him, I was comfortable with asking him to operate. We found that being with fellow church members and other friends provided wonderful encouragement and, we felt, hastened the recovery process.

In retrospect, every decision seemed to have good results.

Even now, more than seven years after the surgery, Deanna and I are elated that I was able to return to my work and finish my vocational career. We give major credit to God the Father, who is in control and who works his work in his kingdom people. Praise God for his love and grace!

Each of you will also face the potential of encountering a malady (perhaps several) as you grow older. In fact, the older you become, the more likely it is that you will experience a chronic or acute illness or an accident. Diseases and accidents are the major factors in our life expectancy.

These are facts of life and not worth worrying about. Can we control them? Of course, but only to a point! We can and should adopt and sustain healthy lifestyles; we can and should be careful at work and play, at home and on the highways of life. But our genetic footprints have been set, and we are products, in significant part, of our forebears.

God the Father has given each of us the propensity for wisdom as well as instructions for responsible living; but, notwithstanding these blessings, he requires that we trust in him completely.

QUESTIONS FOR DISCUSSION

1. First-time, major surgery can be a traumatic experience. If you have had such an experience, reflect

back to the event. Were you aware of God's role in sup-
plying your needs beyond those of medical science?
How can you help another person who is facing a similar situation?

2. What do you feel are the major factors in your
present and future quality of life? Over which of these
do you have significant control?

3. What role is your church currently playing to
help heal its members? What role are you currently playing to help heal your fellow church members?

4. Are you aware of the genetic trends within your
family? How has this awareness influenced your lifestyle
behaviors?

Chapter Seven

TO RETIRE OR NOT TO RETIRE

To retire or not to retire, that is the question. And another one is equally important: Is there life after retirement?

I can answer the second question, but you will have to struggle with the first. I hope that my answer to the last question will give you insight as you wrestle with the first question and make your decision.

There *is* life after retirement, and the quality of that life will depend upon you. As with every stage of life, each of us is individually responsible for the stage called retirement. Up front, I want to give you the best advice I have: If you contemplate retiring, *plan* for it *beforehand!* (The two italicized words are equally important!)

Retirement is a relatively new phenomenon. Essentially nonexistent before the turn of the last century, retirement is becoming a choice for more and more U.S. citizens at earlier and earlier ages. And it may surprise you to realize that these decisions are coming in times when retirement is no longer mandatory.

Before the Age Discrimination in Employment Act (ADEA) became law in 1967, the mandatory age for retirement was sixty-five. The new law meant that an employer could retire any of its employees at age sixty-five, but they could be retained if the employer so chose. In later amendments to the ADEA, that age was elevated to seventy, and in 1986, it was removed entirely. Only a few occupations today require retirement at a specific age.

Interestingly, the average retirement age in the U.S. has dropped to about sixty. When this is coupled with a life expectancy approaching eighty years, some people will spend a quarter of their lives as retirees. That is worth planning for!

PLANNING FOR RETIREMENT

While I cannot advise you as to whether you should retire, should you desire to retire, I have some suggestions for your preretirement planning. The sooner you begin considering these points, the better it should be for you in enjoying a successful retirement.

Five areas are critically important. I will introduce each with a question and follow it with some discussion.

1. IF YOU RETIRE, WHAT WILL YOU DO?

U.S. citizens are, for the most part, *doers!* Remember the old adage, "Don't just stand there; do something"?

Ours is an active culture, and most of us have many "irons in the fire." The thought of going from all of that activity to nothing is quite a fearful prospect.

How do you personally feel about what has been called the Protestant work ethic? Do you agree with many in past generations who believed that the usefulness of persons can be effectively measured *only* in their work? Unfortunately, many who have internalized the work ethic become discouraged to the point of despair when they find themselves outside the workforce at retirement time. Of course their dissatisfaction may result from the fact that they should not have chosen to retire; more likely, however, it results from the fact that they gave little or no consideration to alternatives to their work.

Consider the number 2,340. It is derived this way:

9	hours/day (time spent on one's job, including travel)
X 5	days/week (number of days typically worked each week)
45	hours/week (number of hours on the job each week)
X 52	weeks/year (excluding vacation and holidays)
= 2,340	hours/year (hours spent annually on the job)

When you retire, how will you spend those 2,340 hours each year? I think you will agree that preplanning is necessary. Before you retire, give serious thought to a hobby, volunteer work, a part-time job, travel, and such—all of which should contribute to a successful continuation of life for whatever period of time the Lord chooses to give you.

A growing area of interest for Christians is volunteer missions. Evangelical Christian groups with a conviction and passion for missions are developing increasing opportunities around the world for interested individuals to give from two weeks to two years in this important work.

2. IF YOU RETIRE, HOW WILL YOU FEEL?

Satisfaction during the retirement years will be directly related to one's quality of life in all of life's dimensions (physical, social, psychological, and spiritual). In chapter 3, I reminded us of the importance of good eating and exercise regimens for a healthy body. In chapter 4, I spoke of the problems of encroaching dependence, much of which results from debilitating illnesses.

Right now is a good time to evaluate our lifestyles. If we have begun to sow seeds of sedentary living, we should not be surprised to find we have less energy and vitality in our later years. As with planning for any other aspect of retirement, now is the time to address our health age and begin making changes for the better.

3. IF YOU RETIRE, WITH WHOM WILL YOU RETIRE?

You may be surprised at all of the possible answers to this question. As you consider the ones presented here, you may want to add some others specific to your situation.

Most people will be retiring with their spouse. Given the trends in life expectancy and age at retirement, those of us who have married and successfully sustained that covenant through the years will continue to do so in retirement. Since one or both of you have been working outside the home, you must now consider life with both of you at home. How will you adjust to this new arrangement? I urge you not to assume that things will work out with nary a discouraging word. Rather, I suggest that you brush up on your communication skills and use them for organizing, planning, and so on, to effect a mutually satisfactory arrangement within a household that will be changing significantly.

Consider these changes as creative challenges. Viewing this adjustment as an opportunity rather than a necessary evil will help get you well on your way to positive experiences.

Beyond the likelihood of retiring with your spouse, what is the possibility of retiring with your children? Ordinarily, your children are grown and gone from home when you retire, and you have already adjusted to the "empty nest." But what of the "boomerang" child? What if you have a child who, because of a failed marriage, lost job, or some other reason, asks to move in with you? That isn't what you expected, is it? Of course not! Nevertheless, this is a situation that some prospective retirees are facing.

Another possibility is that you will retire with your parent(s) or your spouse's parent(s). (This thought probably occurred to you as you read chap. 4.) If you retire around age sixty, what is the likelihood that your parent(s) will be alive? Looking after their changing needs could occupy a considerable part of your time. Such an eventuality should be factored into your plans.

Finally, what about your grandchildren? Will you retire with them? You are probably thinking, *I hope so!*—meaning, "I'd like to be close enough to my grandchildren to be with them often and return them to their parents after we've had our time together." This surely is the ideal for most grandparents.

However, what if your child cannot or will not care for his/her own children? What if your child and grandchild move back to your home and then your child moves out, leaving the grandchild with you? Would you feel responsible for a grandchild who is not being cared for or who is otherwise being neglected?

Several years ago, my pastor and I invited a former professor of ours to come to our church for Senior Adult Day. He was semiretired at the time and was able to come for two days.

When he arrived with his wife, two young boys accompanied them; one was ten years old and the other was eight. The boys were the couple's grandchildren, whom they had recently adopted. They explained that their daughter, the mother of the boys, was mentally incompetent and incapable of raising her children. They asked that we pray for them to have enough years left to raise those boys to adulthood. Then they added, "Our daughter just gave birth to a beautiful daughter. We do not know what to do to help in this situation. Please pray for our daughter and for us."

Unfortunately, these types of situations seem to be increasing in our society. This is why question 3 is so critically important.

4. If you retire, with what will you retire?

Most people believe this to be the most important question of all. The "what" of the question means finances, and certainly it is a very important consideration. Still, don't be duped by the notion that many have expressed: "If I have my finances in order, retirement will be a breeze!" Not necessarily! There are many financially-secure retirees out there who are quite unhappy.

The following steps should help you as you make your financial arrangements:

A. Compile a list of your assets. (See chap. 5.)
B. Estimate your expenses in retirement. Do not let this suggestion appear daunting. Checklists are available to help you think about your usual expense items. You will not be able to be exact, but you can develop a reasonably accurate figure.

C. Estimate your retirement income (sources and amounts). Most of you will have a pension through your employer as well as Social Security benefits. Accurate, projected estimates can be secured from your employer's pension manager and from the Social Security Administration. In fact, the latter makes periodic estimates and mails them automatically to all subscribers.

D. Compare estimated expenses with estimated income. If your estimated expenses exceed your estimated income, you need to begin an investment program (the sooner, the better) and/or find ways to reduce your expenses in retirement. If estimated income exceeds estimated expenses, you will want to inflation-protect your fixed-income(s) as well as your new investments.

E. Estimate the length of time to be spent in retirement. I can see you smiling as you read this because none of us knows how long we will live. Nevertheless, the question related to this suggestion is this: "For how long will your retirement income need to last?" A good investment strategy would be to have your income last into perpetuity, which would mean that you will not become financially dependent upon anyone. In addition, you would have something to leave in your estate.

It is your responsibility to see that you do not run out of money. An obvious way to help this happen is to consider your expected lifestyle in retirement. You may wish to develop and maintain a more modest lifestyle.

F. Secure a financial adviser. If you need help dealing with your findings from the above steps, find an adviser to help you with investments, management of your financial portfolio, and a strategy to inflation-proof your fixed incomes.

5. IF YOU RETIRE, WHERE WILL YOU LIVE?

Most U.S. citizens stay put at retirement. About three-quarters of our retirees stay where they have been living. Of those who move, most relocate within the same community. Only about 5 percent undertake a major relocation (i.e., some distance away).

If you were asked to close your eyes and imagine your "dream house" in retirement, where would it be? Would it be your present home, another home in a nearby place, or a place some distance from where you now live? Your success in retirement may be determined in part by your answer to these questions.

Sociologists sometimes speak of "push-pull" factors as regards our physical mobility (which is considerable in our society; it is estimated that as many as 20 percent of our population change residences every year).

"Push" factors are those conditions, situations, and such, that make people generally dissatisfied where they are. These factors serve to push people away from such locations. "Pull" factors are those things that serve to draw people to other places: a better climate, lower cost of living, more exciting opportunities, lower crime rate, and so forth.

You may be pleased with where you are (most people seem to be), but if you aren't sure, I suggest that you make a list of your own push-pull factors. If you are really serious about relocating, investigate those important items at the place(s) you might wish to live. Several publications are available that rate various geographical locations here and abroad on a number of critical factors.

A Personal Word

Because I have been conducting preretirement planning seminars for the past fifteen years, I have tried to "practice what I've been preaching." In this chapter I have given you the essence of what I cover in these seminars, but you may wonder how it has worked for me.

I retired five years ago after having tried to follow the advice I have given to several hundred seminar participants. Here are a few of my experiences:

When Deanna and I began asking each other, "What shall we do to replace 2,340 hours a year?" we felt that we needed both *individual* and *together* answers. Before retiring I took several classes in stained glass design and construction, and I decided to increase my time on the golf course. We talked about traveling together—for missions opportunities and for personal edification. A two-week mission trip to Hungary with Campus Crusade for Christ was planned and executed, with wonderful experiences and fond memories. On our way home from Budapest, we took an extra ten days and visited the air base where we had been stationed in Germany in 1961–62. We then drove into Switzerland and Italy before returning to Frankfurt to fly home.

Since retiring, Deanna has developed a writing ministry. She designs her own cards, using photos she has made in our environs. She writes cards and letters almost daily to folks we know who need encouragement, affirmation, healing, and such.

The most exciting revelation for us has been to see how God continues to utilize the spiritual gifts he gave us. Soon after we retired and relocated, we were asked to "help" at a girl's ranch, a facility for disadvantaged, troubled youth. Deanna was asked to teach the elementary girls, and I was asked to tutor high-school algebra. This was less remarkable for Deanna, who is retired from elementary teaching; but it was most remarkable for me, a retired gerontology professor. However, my undergraduate degree, taken forty-three years ago, was in mathematics. I knew that God had orchestrated this opportunity, for it never would have occurred to me!

We live in northern New Mexico, in the Sangre de Christo range of the Rocky Mountains, at an altitude of 7,500 feet above sea level. A circumference road around our area is two miles in distance, and most mornings I walk this route in about thirty minutes. My family physician has encouraged this aerobic exercise, and it certainly helps me feel more vigorous. While both my wife and I have added a few pounds since retiring, we work hard to keep weight gain under control.

Six months prior to our retirement in 1997, Deanna's mother passed away at age eighty-six. Almost three years earlier, her father had died at ninety-two. Both of my parents were eighty-three when we retired, but Dad was already experiencing some early signs of congestive heart failure.

In a real sense, we retired with my parents. While they were living independently, my brother and I shared a deep sense of responsibility for monitoring their well-being. A little more than a year ago, Dad began to fail rather rapidly. On January 31, 2001, Deanna and I returned to Texas to care for Dad, along with the local hospice organization whom his physician had recommended that we engage. A week later, Dad passed away.

In the ensuing four months, we got Mom relocated to an apartment in a retirement center. She, my brother, and I made this choice together, and she has adjusted to widowhood and single living remarkably well. In the meantime, I executed Dad's will, we had a "moving" sale of their dispensable belongings, and we sold the house in which they had lived.

These times were quite difficult, for none of us had passed this way before, but we saw God's hand of grace and love through it all.

Regarding financial arrangements, every person will be located somewhere along a wide spectrum of possibilities. What Deanna and I recall from the list of steps I presented earlier are steps A, B, and C:

A. List of assets. I cannot overemphasize the importance of this task. Please review my discussion in chapter 5 and try to do this right away.

B. Estimate your expenses. I spent one long evening (5–6 hours) on this task, and I have discovered that my estimations have been quite accurate. Arriving at a "ballpark" figure is essential; otherwise you cannot estimate the adequacy of your retirement income. As you work on your expenses (items and amounts), you will probably have several question marks that call for you to seek further information. Don't allow yourself to procrastinate at this point.

C. Estimate your income(s). Do it right now or no later than tomorrow! Call your employer's pension manager for an appointment. You will probably have half-a-dozen options for receiving your benefits. Which will be best for you? Now is the time to begin considering all possibilities. Contact your local Social Security office and ask for an estimation of benefits *with projections* (i.e., what will my benefits be __ years from now?). I began investigating these income options several years in advance of my retirement, and I felt much more confident when the time came. Making estimate of both expenses and incomes does not produce certainties, but it produces confidences.

As you plan for your retirement consider the five essential questions: (1) What will you do? (2) How will you feel? (3) With whom will you retire? (4) With what will you retire? and (5) Where will you live? One or more of these questions should "ring your bell" if you have no ready answers. If you are contemplating retirement, begin working and planning in those areas where you have obvious needs. You may wish to ask your employer (human resources manager) to offer a preretirement planning seminar.

QUESTIONS FOR DISCUSSION

1. Many people express a desire to continue indefinitely with their employment. Many others are equally desirous to retire as soon as they can. If these two types

represent the extremes on a continuum, where would you place yourself along that continuum? What help do you need now to decide whether or not (and when) you should retire? Where will you go for that help?

2. Only a handful of major corporations in the United States offer a full-fledged preretirement planning seminar for their employees. Most seem to think their pension plan is an adequate "perk" for their workers. If you have asked your employer to host such a seminar but to no avail, how about asking your church to arrange one for your members?

3. As you reflect on the five areas discussed in this chapter, which of these do you feel you should begin investigating now? Will you make it a joint effort with your spouse?

Chapter Eight

GETTING PAST THE BUREAUCRATS

My work for fifteen years as director of the geron-tology program at a state university was both ful-filling and frustrating.

It was rewarding from the standpoint of our stu-dents, who were either majors or minors in gerontology and who, in either case, were required to complete a one-hundred-clock-hour internship. Being placed in an agency delivering services to the elderly in the commu-nity afforded them valuable practical experiences, including a good look at what working with the elderly would be like. It also established an interfacing network between our university and those community organiza-tions that focused on the aged. An enduring partnership developed that met the needs of three interrelated groups of people: the students, the elderly, and the community.

But amidst all this activity was the frustration with the fact that too many of our senior citizens were "falling through the cracks." At least weekly, and sometimes more often, we discovered people with needs who were unaware of the services available. This chapter is designed to provide information and awareness that, if known and used, will help match needs and services.

THE OLDER AMERICANS ACT (OAA)

The Older Americans Act of 1965 created a national network for the planning, coordination, and delivery of services to the elderly (aged sixty and over). It also established State Units of Aging (SUAs), which in turn designates local Area Agencies of Aging (AAAs) that administer the local service plans. Through the AAAs, local service providers implement the following programs:

- information and referral
- transportation
- homemaker services
- adult day care
- nutrition education
- congregate meals
- legal services
- respite (relief) care
- senior centers

The senior centers act as hubs for a variety of activities and opportunities for senior adults during each weekday. Seniors come to play games, learn crafts, enjoy entertainment, visit and reminisce, and enjoy a hot, nutritious meal together at noon.

At the senior center in my town, I worked with the director to bring my gerontology students in to "adopt" a grandparent. At the beginning of the semester, my students and I traveled to the center during our class period. We met and paired off with either an individual or a couple and planned to meet with them periodically throughout a four-and-a-half-month semester. These meetings were mutually arranged, based on activities and time constraints. Typically, these student-grandparent(s) groups would visit, shop, have a meal, go to a movie, and the like. At semester end, we returned to the senior center and hosted a party for our grandparents: in the fall, we had a Christmas party, and in the spring, we enjoyed a May picnic.

These activities were to us, and we think to the elders as well, added bonuses of having a senior center in a university town. For most, these "assigned" relationships lasted just for the semester, but for some, they flourished into lasting friendships. A few endured well beyond the student's graduation. I suspect that some of these pairs are still communicating.

This is just one example of how many senior adults have found a transformation from loneliness to meaningfulness by participating in available programs. Thus,

Title III of the Older Americans Act, the single federal social service entity that is designed specifically for older people, has exemplified government at its best! But only if those for whom it is designed know about it and choose to take advantage of it.

While enormous amounts of time, effort, and money have been poured into establishing this network of needed services, of what value are they if a significant part of the targeted population is unaware of them? Worse still, what about those who are aware and needy but choose not to avail themselves of these services?

SENIORS WHO DON'T KNOW
ABOUT AVAILABLE GOVERNMENT SERVICES

Ignorance is an unpleasant word, but only when critically applied. We all are ignorant as we consider the vastness of God's creation and realize that our knowledge of his universe(s) is miniscule. But, to our credit, we seek to know; and we add to our knowledge daily.

The rub here is our ignorance about available knowledge for which we have a need. As a senior adult or as one caring for a senior adult, you need to know the information available about the Older Americans Act. You also need to know about Social Security and about the aging process. You need to know whatever information is available about the changes you are experiencing.

I mentioned earlier that a major component of the

Older Americans Act focuses on information and referral. Early on, the framers of this legislation recognized the need to inform and make referrals to and for potential subscribers to the services. This has been done primarily through public service announcements in the media—newspapers, television, radio, and so forth. It has also been done with bulletins posted in places frequented by the elderly and at periodic events (health fairs, jamborees, etc.) sponsored for senior citizens.

Despite these concerted efforts, too many still have not gotten the word. Obviously, the needy elderly and those caring for them also have a responsibility to seek out whatever may be available for them. Potential recipients of needed services must take the initiative to ask what, when, how, and so forth.

I have used the Older Americans Act so far in this discussion. What about the Social Security system? Most of you who read these words are, or will be, receiving some income support from that bureaucratic agency of the federal government. Do you know all that you need to know about its various programs? I'm not speaking of its history or of the nuts and bolts of how the system works, but what will your benefits be and how will they be determined?

A significant part of the preretirement seminar I teach (see chap. 7) includes a presentation by a representative of the Social Security Administration. I have learned, as I have listened to participant questions and responses for more than fifteen years, that fundamental knowledge is generally lacking. The good news is that the information needed is readily available. By contacting your local Social Security office or calling the Social Security Administration's toll-free 800 number, you can find answers to such questions as:

- When am I eligible to begin receiving retirement benefits?
- What documents do I need to demonstrate my eligibility?
- What reduction in benefits will I have if I request benefits early?
- What is meant by the "pension-offset" that I've heard about?
- How are my benefits affected by those of my spouse?
- Will my benefits be taxable?

In 1965, the Social Security Act of 1935 was amended to provide health insurance for the elderly. It is called Medicare, and it consists of two components: Part A, a *compulsory* hospital insurance, and Part B, a *voluntary* supplementary medical insurance that helps pay doctors, outpatient benefits, home health services, and such. Those who opt for Part B must pay a monthly premium (fifty-two dollars in 2002).

Unless you have an unusual situation, a Social Security representative can process your questions rather quickly. Still, it is your responsibility to go and ask, and it is your responsibility to ascertain that your records in their computer are correct.

SENIORS WHO DON'T CARE ABOUT SOME AVAILABLE GOVERNMENT SERVICES

Some elderly folks have an attitude problem. Let me explain. I am not speaking of all seniors who choose not to participate in the services offered in their local senior center. Some are too busy—they are still working full-time, or they are retired, having planned beforehand for adequate activities to replace their work. These folks are neither lonely nor bored.

The seniors of whom I speak are those who are bored and/or lonely—usually because they haven't planned well for their retirement, and "the ole rockin' chair's got 'em!" But let a family member or friend suggest the senior center, and they say, "I don't want to go to that place with all those old people sitting around giving organ recitals [meaning, telling which of their internal organs are not working properly]."

In most cases, these naysayers are like the little boy who didn't like squash. He had never tasted it, but he knew he didn't like it. Similarly, these poor-attitude seniors have never been to the senior center, but they have "heard" about it.

As if making a decision against something without any hard evidence isn't bad enough, there are other older adults who say, "Those people [at the senior center] are beneath my station; I'm not interested in associating with them." This is a truly tragic attitude, for it is un-Christian! But as I pointed out in chapter 2, prejudicial attitudes and their attendant behaviors breed from ignorance, misinformation, and inexperience.

SUMMARY

Though we all occasionally have had unpleasant experiences dealing with some bureaucratic organizations, I suspect that such encounters have had more to do with the personality of the individual bureaucrat than with the nature of the organization. Thus, I encourage both patience and persistence. When you need to contact an agency in your local aging network, Social Security office, or other governmental entity, you will most likely speak to a helpful, caring individual. Occasionally you may speak to a representative who is more businesslike than cordial. Don't be discouraged. Instead, be persistent and maintain your calm demeanor. The spirit of the Golden Rule will always serve you well.

I close this chapter with another gentle reminder. We have all heard that "the only foolish question is the one that is never asked." In like fashion, if you have a need and an organization is available to meet that need, your reluctance to pursue it is also foolish. "He who asks not, receives not," and he who hesitates may also lose out.

Questions for Discussion

1. *Bureaucratic red tape* and *bureaucratic run-around* are pejorative terms sometimes associated with large public and private organizations due to perceived inefficiencies. Are such generalizations fairly made? How do we know that our individual difficulties with such organizations represent the organization as a whole? Are you employed by a bureaucratic organization? If so, are you a typical or an atypical bureaucrat?

2. Are you (or do you know) a needy and/or lonely senior adult? What initiatives have you taken to get recognized needs met? To whom have you expressed your dissatisfaction when your needs have not been fairly met?

3. Have you met any senior adults who have an attitude problem (e.g., haughtiness, condescending to others, etc.)? Are any such folks in your church? If so, how might the church deal with them in loving but effective ways?

Chapter Nine

THE SPIRITUAL DIMENSION

Earlier I spoke of life as a journey, an exciting odyssey for us as we make our pilgrimage with God. Throughout this journey we have experienced both difficulties and joys, and such experiences will continue. We will also continue to try to make sense of them all. We are at least vaguely aware that much of what happens to us is predicated by our designs and choices, yet our sovereign God is intimately involved in our affairs. He is a hands-on God. At divers and appropriate times he intervenes, and we feel his holy presence. In response we rejoice, offering praise and thanks. Still, much of our time is marked with humdrum routine, and unless we are careful, we will become wearied by it all.

We move along in life—sometimes plodding, sometimes skipping, sometimes running until we are exhausted. We know that God has called us, and we look forward to his final destination for us. In the meantime, however, we know that there is an important process involved before we reach that destination.

In chapter 1, I discussed three important aspects of the aging process: the physiological, the psychological, and the social. I also mentioned a fourth dimension— the spiritual—that distinguishes us from others of God's creatures. All four aspects are constantly changing, and all four—combined and interacting—represent who we are. I don't know if the first three dimensions are eternal, but the spiritual dimension certainly is. Therefore it is most important in defining who we are.

In this chapter, I will develop several criteria that should help us see something of the vastness of each individual's spiritual self.

CREATOR AND CREATURE: THE IMPORTANCE OF GOD IN THE EQUATION OF MAN

God is completely eternal—he had no beginning, and he has no ending. God also is changeless. He is completely perfect, completely holy, completely righteous. He is just that: complete! He has no need to change. The writer of Psalm 102 must have taken great comfort in the eternal and changeless nature of God:

> In the beginning you laid the foundations
>   of the earth,

and the heavens are the work of your hands.
They will perish, but you remain;
   they will all wear out like a garment.
Like clothing you will change them
   and they will be discarded.
But you remain the same,
   and your years will never end. (vv. 25–27)

Jesus Christ, who is God, also is changeless. The writer of the Epistle to the Hebrews quoted the same three verses from Psalm 102 when he described the Father's work through the Son (see Heb. 1:10–12).

In contrast to the changelessness of the Godhead, we creatures of God are constantly changing. Even so, the Creator has given us an eternal nature. Though we had a beginning, we will have no ending. The teacher of Ecclesiastes put it this way: "He [God] has made everything beautiful in its time. He has also set eternity in the hearts of men; yet they cannot fathom what God has done from beginning to end" (3:11). I see this as our spiritual dimension—we are finite beings with an infinite quality.

The term I like best to describe spiritual change is "to become." Humans are changing because they need to change; they need to become the new creatures God wishes them to be. Consider these exhortations from Scripture:

1. Humans need to change from (to put off) their carnal (fleshly) nature. Paul wrote to the believers in Ephesus: "You were taught, with regard to your former way of life, to put off your old self, which is being corrupted by its deceitful desires; to be made new in the attitude of your minds" (Eph. 4:22–23). He used different words to make a similar appeal to the church at Colosse (Col. 3:5, 8–9).

2. Humans need to transform (renew) their minds. Writing to the church at Rome, Paul urged the brothers: "Do not conform any longer to the pattern of this world, but be transformed by the renewing of your mind" (Rom. 12:2a).

3. Humans need to repent (change direction) when they sin. Luke quoted Jesus, who was preaching to a large crowd: "Do you think that these Galileans were worse sinners than all the other Galileans because they suffered this way? I tell you, no! But unless you repent, you too will all perish" (Luke 13:2–3). When Peter was preaching to the crowd on the day of Pentecost, he said, "Repent and be baptized, every one of you, in the name of Jesus Christ for the forgiveness of your sins" (Acts 2:38a).

4. Humans need to become righteous. Jesus told the crowd on the mountainside: "Seek first his kingdom and his righteousness, and all these things

will be given to you as well" (Matt. 6:33). Paul reminded the Christians at Corinth: "God made him who had no sin to be sin for us, so that in him we might become the righteousness of God" (2 Cor. 5:21).

5. Humans need to spend time in God's written Word. When Joshua became the leader of the Israelites following the death of Moses, God said to him, "Do not let this Book of the Law depart from your mouth; meditate on it day and night, so that you may be careful to do everything written in it" (Josh. 1:8a). Later the psalmist wrote, "Oh, how I love your law! I meditate on it all day long. . . . Your word is a lamp to my feet and a light for my path" (Ps. 119:97, 105).

These are but a few examples from God's Word, which is replete with charges for us to exercise our volitional nature rightly rather than wrongly and obediently rather than disobediently. Our "becoming," according to God's will, means maturing in godliness and growing in Christlikeness.

FEARS AND TRUST

Life is often beset with difficulties, which, in turn, may spawn worries and fears. We should expect difficulties, but fears and worries are unbecoming to believers. Jesus admonished us not to worry (see Matt. 6:25–34). It

may seem trite to say that our fears are a matter of mis-
trust—but they are! Nevertheless, since we all are sometimes victims of fear, further insight might be helpful.

Several years ago I was invited to preach at a church
in a nearby town. It was the evening of Senior Adult Day,
and I wrote a sermon that addressed some of the fears of
older people. Using the story of David and Goliath, I suggested that items focused on in our "What if?" syn-
dromes are like giants in our lives. For example, a senior
adult might ask one or more of the following questions:

- What if *I become dependent?*
- What if *my spouse dies?*
- What if *I contract Alzheimer's disease?*
- What if _____?

When we verbalize such questions, we find ourselves
in a situation similar to the Israelites' as they encountered the Philistines and Goliath (see 1 Sam. 17). We can
either sell out to fear (as Saul and his army did) or go
forth to meet the adversary (as David did).

In "Ugly Gremlins,"[1] Jodie Yoder cited Verna
Birkley, who wrote about a woman named Jo. At age
seventy-two Jo was worried about growing older. Her
worries specifically included:

- becoming a widow
- suffering a long illness
- ending up in a nursing home
- becoming senile.

Her "ugly gremlins" were like my "giants of despair." But what does God tell us about growing older? "They will still bear fruit in old age; they will stay fresh and green" (Ps. 92:14). Shouldn't God's promise be good enough for us? Trusting God is our only hope for our fears and worries. What's more, it is *essential* for a healthy spiritual life!

CONTENTMENT

For our later years to be the best that they can be, we must discover and embrace the joy of contentment. In his "Epistle of Joy" (the letter to the Philippians), Paul wrote from prison about his thankfulness to God and his partnership with the Philippians in the gospel of Christ (Phil. 1:4–5). His had been an extraordinary pilgrimage with the Lord, beginning with his remarkable, life-transforming experience years earlier on the road to Damascus. As Paul was nearing the end of physical life, perhaps he was reflecting on his journey and sharing some summary advice.

He might have chronicled some of his experiences, as he had done in 2 Corinthians 11:16–33, but he simply reminded his fellow Christians that he had "learned to be content whatever the circumstances: whether in need or with plenty, whether well fed or hungry, I can do everything through him who gives me strength" (Phil. 4:11b–13, paraphrased).

Contentment is a state of mind that evidences a simple, childlike trust in God. Consider Kevin, whose story came from my daughter-in-law just a few days ago through E-mail. Kevin is a six-foot-two, thirty-year-old man with the mind of a seven-year-old boy. His mental impairment, according to his family, resulted from complications at birth. Kevin's brother tells his story:

I remember wondering if Kevin realizes he is different. Is he ever dissatisfied with his monotonous life? Up before dawn each day, off to work at a workshop for the disabled, home to walk our cocker spaniel, returning to eat his favorite macaroni and cheese for dinner, and later to bed. The only variation in the entire scheme are laundry days, when he hovers excitedly over the washing machine like a mother with her newborn child. He does not seem dissatisfied. He lopes out to the bus every morning at 7:05, eager for a day of simple work. He wrings his hands excitedly while the water boils on the stove before dinner, and he stays up late twice a week to gather our dirty laundry for his next day's laundry chores.

And Saturdays—oh, the bliss of Saturdays! That's the day my dad takes Kevin to the airport to have a soft drink, watch the planes land, and speculate loudly on the destination of each passenger inside. "That one's goin' to Chi-car-go!"

Kevin shouts as he claps his hands. His anticipation is so great he can hardly sleep on Friday nights. I don't think Kevin knows anything exists outside his world of daily rituals and weekend field trips. He doesn't know what it means to be discontent. His life is simple. He will never know the entanglements of wealth or power, and he does not care what brand of clothing he wears or what kind of food he eats. He recognizes no differences in people, treating each person as an equal and a friend.

His needs have always been met, and he never worries that one day they may not be. His hands are diligent. Kevin is never so happy as when he is working. When he unloads the dishwasher or vacuums the carpet, his heart is completely in it. He does not shrink from a job when it is begun, and he does not leave a job until it is finished. But when his tasks are done, Kevin knows how to relax. He is not obsessed with his work or the work of others. His heart is pure. He still believes everyone tells the truth, promises must be kept, and when you are wrong, you apologize instead of argue. Free from pride and unconcerned with appearances, Kevin is not afraid to cry when he is hurt, angry or sorry. He is always transparent, always sincere. And he trusts God.

Here is a man-boy who is content. We probably feel pity for Kevin, but don't we also feel a longing to be so trusting and pure? I believe that God can give us this kind of trust, and with it we can rise above the skepticism and pride that often come from relying too much on education and intellectual reasoning.

Though the native intelligence of Kevin and the apostle Paul are incomparable, their state of contentment is very similar. It's a matter of trust!

GOD'S CALLING, OUR FRUITFULNESS

And we know that in all things God works for the good of those who love him, who have been *called* according to his purpose. For those God foreknew he also predestined to be conformed to the likeness of his Son, that he might be the firstborn among many brothers. And those he predestined, he also *called;* those he *called,* he also justified; those he justified, he also glorified. (Rom. 8:28–30, emphasis mine)

The context of the term *call* in this passage means "to invite or to summon," and implicit within this context is a corresponding enabling. Thus God calls us

- to be his people (Titus 2:14)
- to receive (rather than to reject) his Son (John 1:11–12)

- to be parts of Christ's Body (the Church) (Eph. 4:4–6)
- to live a life worthy of this calling (Eph. 4:1)
- to make our calling sure (2 Pet. 1:10)
- to be fruitful (John 15:1–17)

The hymn writers of the Old Testament often sang of righteousness, noting that fruitfulness is inherent in righteousness. In the first psalm, for example, it is the righteous who are like "a tree planted by streams of water, which yield its fruit in season and whose leaf does not wither" (Ps. 1:3). Earlier I cited a verse from Psalm 92: "They will still bear fruit in old age, they will stay fresh and green" (v. 14). Who are "they"? The answer is in verses 12 and 13: "The righteous will flourish like a palm tree, they will grow like a cedar of Lebanon; planted in the house of the LORD, they will flourish in the courts of our God."

The writer of Psalm 71 calls upon God for refuge and hope and then praises God for his righteousness:

Do not cast me away when I am old;
     do not forsake me when my strength is gone. . . .
My mouth will tell of your righteousness,
     of your salvation all day long,
     though I know not its measure.
I will come and proclaim your mighty acts,
     O Sovereign LORD;
     I will proclaim your righteousness, yours alone.

114 ~ AGING GRACEFULLY

> Since my youth, O God, you have taught me,
>   and to this day I declare your marvelous deeds.
> Even when I am old and gray,
>   do not forsake me, O God,
> till I declare your power to the next generation,
>   your might to all who are to come. (vv. 9,
>   15–18)

In this psalm, our fruitfulness is in proclamation, in declaring God's mighty deeds and telling the following generations of his transforming power. Such testifying is part of God's plan for others to know him.

In chapter 7, we discussed the topic of retirement, but what does that mean in light of God's call to us?

Though we addressed the notion of retiring from one's employment, God also calls us to *his* work, from which we should *never* retire! While our career is part of doing God's work, it is not the whole. Consider these two suggestions:

1. Though it is entirely appropriate to retire from a particular position of service to the Lord, it is never appropriate to retire from doing God's work altogether.

2. Instead of considering retiring *from* something, consider retiring *to* something.

These two thoughts are critical to our spiritual pilgrimage, so let me briefly develop each.

Some of us may have become enmeshed in the unfortunate dichotomy of distinguishing callings in terms of sacred and secular. According to this way of thinking, a person is "called by God" to a sacred (church-related, etc.) position, but in contrast, another person "chooses" to take a secular position. The implications are obvious—one is "better" than the other. The truth is that God calls us to whatever he calls us, and he equips (enables) us to do that job well—for his glory. God used Peter, Andrew, James, and John when they were fishing for fish as well as for men. He used Paul when he was making tents as well as when he was planting churches and writing letters from prison.

If you are struggling with the question of retiring, you may be asking, "How can I think of retiring from what God has called me to do?" Unfortunately, many of God's formerly effective servants have stayed too long in a particular position. The changing effects of aging have caused a decline in energy, if not enthusiasm, and these faithful servants are laboring where they need not. The better question for them would be: "To what can I retire so as to continue to be fruitful for my Lord?"

Not long ago I read a devotional written by David Roper. He said this about "Old Timers": "We tend to lose heart as we age. Our physical strength abates; our health deteriorates; our memory gets cloudy. But we

need not despair. Every day can be a new beginning
toward 'good old age.' Getting older can mean growing,
maturing, ministering, venturing—enjoying life to the
end of our days."[2]

Dale Gallagher recently wrote in a similar vein
regarding our continuing effectiveness for the Lord. Her
poem is called "Am I Too Old?"

> Am I too old to serve my Lord?
> Am I too old to sing His praise?
> Am I too old to teach His Word
> Or spread the Word in other ways?
>
> If each day brings me closer to Him,
> If each song lifts my heart in prayer,
> If God's own Spirit leads me onward,
> How can age cause me despair?
>
> Some saw Peter speak to others,
> His confidence in Christ shined through.
> They realized that he had been
> With Jesus, and it had made him new.
>
> May I so shine with Jesus' power
> So others look at me and say,
> "She has truly seen the Savior,
> She has been with Him today."[3]

Be encouraged, fellow pilgrims, for you know that you are never too old to serve, to sing, to teach, to pray, to work for the Lord. He has called you to *his* work, not just to a position. Let us always inquire of the Lord (see 2 Sam. 5:19) and follow his leading. And let us all be "confident of this, that he who began a good work in you will carry it on to completion until the day of Christ Jesus" (Phil. 1:6).

SELF-EXAMINATION

Throughout one's life journey, and especially when one is on mission with God, continuing self-examination is of utmost importance. We often reflect on the question, "How am I doing?" as regards our job performance, our relationships with supervisors and peers, and our career objectives. Shouldn't similar self-assessments also attend our relationships with God, family, and others?

What does God require of us? His answer through Micah was: "To act justly and to love mercy and to walk humbly with your God" (Micah 6:8b). Our God has lofty expectations for his people, and these expectations are related to who we are spiritually.

Knowing who we are and *whose* we are will be reflected in our relationships, so I recommend that we look often at our relationships with the following:

1. *God.* He is our first priority—the linchpin for all other relationships. He is our Creator, Redeemer, and Sustainer. Therefore, let us ask ourselves these questions:

- What is my relationship now with God the Son, in whom I have right standing with God the Father?
- What is my relationship with God the Holy Spirit? Have I sought, found, and appropriated his special gift(s) for me? Do I regularly exhibit his fruits (see Gal. 5:22–23)? Do I invite him to walk beside me as Comforter and Intercessor?

2. *Family.* No human relationships are more important than those associated with our family—nuclear and extended. God's first intentions and directives regarding the human family are given in Genesis 2: "For this reason a man will leave his father and mother and be united to his wife, and they will become one flesh" (v. 24). In this one verse, God calls for monogamy (one spouse), heterosexuality (one man and one woman), and a cleaving to one's spouse in terms of primary (but not exclusive) focus.

In my view, spousal relationships are the second-most important of all relationships, and the third-most important are parent-child relationships. Therefore, we do well to examine our responsibilities and commitments to family members.

3. *Church.* The church, universal and local, is ordained of God as the chief caring community. Our Lord told Peter that he would build his Church on Peter's confession that "you [Jesus] are the Christ, the Son of the living God" (Matt. 16:16). Paul later wrote to

the church at Corinth: "God has arranged the parts in the body, every one of them, just as he wanted them to be" (1 Cor. 12:18). We are, or should be, in the church at God's behest, and our relationships with fellow believers and potential members should demand much care and cultivation. The ongoing question for self-examination should be this: "How am I contributing to unity and harmony in my church?"

4. *Other humans.* Every person that we meet—incidentally or on a recurring basis—is a child of God and a real or potential member of his kingdom. Every encounter at work, in the marketplace, on an airplane, in a neighborly visit, and such, should be considered a divine appointment. How then do we meet people? Pleasantly, with a smile; cautiously, with hesitation or suspicion; sourly, with bitterness or cynicism? The first impression we give to others can make a world of difference for future opportunities. It can create or perpetuate prejudices about us as individuals *and* about those whom we represent.

Our spiritual dimension is multifaceted and complex. It is difficult to fully apprehend because it is constantly changing. Nevertheless, it represents who we are at every stage—every moment—of life as it interfaces with all other aspects of self.

QUESTIONS FOR DISCUSSION

1. How do you understand God's call on your life? How is your call related to your transformation (an unbeliever becoming a believer)?

2. Are your spiritual changes in life related to the changes in the other dimensions (physiological, psychological, and social) of your life? Which of these changes are most important to you? Why?

3. What fears beset your life? How are you handling them?

4. What are the differences between the "gifts" and the "fruits" of the Holy Spirit? Do you know your spiritual gift (or gifts)?

5. How do you understand the following two statements found in this chapter?

A. "No human relationships are more important than those associated with our family."

B. "Spousal relationships are the second-most important of all relationships, and the third-most important are parent-child relationships."

What is *the most important* of all relationships? Why?

Chapter Ten

COMMENCEMENT

For eight exciting years I was privileged to direct an Elderhostel program at the university where I taught. When we joined the network, Elderhostel was in its infancy: its programs were one week in length; each offered three minicourses; it was becoming national in scope (having begun as a regional program in New England); and most of the sponsoring institutions were colleges and universities. Now, after more than a quarter-century of experience, there are multiple-week offerings, many of the studies are longer and more extensive, host institutions are much more varied, and there is an expanding international focus.

From the outset, Elderhostel national leaders strongly recommended that no courses be offered on the topics of death and dying. "They won't fly!" was the chief argument. "Too morbid!" was the explanation. I accepted their contention without question and dutifully offered courses that would be both interesting and uplifting. But I was scratching my head all the while, for during those years our university offered a course to our students called "Sociology of Death and Dying," and we filled those classes every semester. Did this mean that college students weren't reluctant to tackle the topic of death, but older adults were afraid to talk about it?

In this final chapter, I want to bring these topics to your attention. I think it is essential to recognize the fact that as we are growing older, we also are dying—physically, of course; hopefully not spiritually. As I asked in chapter 1, "How are you dealing with your aging?" I ask now, "How are you dealing with your dying?" Death is God-ordained; indeed he gives us ample indications of this fact in his written Word (c.f., 2 Kings 14:6; Eccles. 3:2; Heb. 9:27; and Rom. 6:23). Death, like aging, is both inevitable and irresistible.

Dealing with death and dying is healthy; denying or suppressing these realities is unhealthy. In fact, denial creates the worst kind of "giant of despair" in our lives. While facing death head-on with courage may not be easy, it is possible (see Ps. 23:4). I hope the following discussions will help you do this.

TERMINOLOGY AND MEANING

The term *death* may be described from at least two perspectives. Physiologically, it means the cessation of life, the permanent shutting-down of all bodily systems and functions. Spiritually, it is viewed as the transition of one's spirit from the temporality of physical life into eternity.

The term *dying* refers to a process that may be viewed several ways: over a period of time, through a series of events or stages, as a kind of trajectory, etcetera, until death comes.

While many people express uncertainty and ambivalence regarding death, some say that they have a fear, not so much of death, but of the dying process. This concern seems to center on the notion that dying may be accompanied by pain and suffering. You probably have heard some folks say, "If I had my preference, I'd rather die quickly than suffer through a lengthy illness." I call this mind-set the "Bing Crosby Syndrome." The term is mine, so you've never heard it before. I coined the term to describe those people who remember that the former crooner dropped dead as he walked off a golf course in Spain. I have heard many such folks say, "Boy, that's how I'd like to go!"

But we do not orchestrate our death. If we did, we would need to remind ourselves that the issue of death does not involve only the one who dies; it also involves those who are left behind grieving. Should we have a concern for them? Absolutely! Therefore, let us remember that our sudden death would be a true shock for our family and friends.

GOD SPEAKS ABOUT DEATH

Is death an end or a beginning, or is it both? Is graduation from high school or college an end or a beginning, or is it both? I believe we can make a case for all of these being correct answers—it is simply a matter of perspective.

Christians speak of dying and going to heaven. My study Bible defines heaven as "the eternal dwelling place of God and the redeemed"[1] (see 2 Cor. 5:1–5). Thus, at death we *end* physical life and *begin* (commence) eternal life. Consequently for the believer, death represents a transition from this world to the next, and with this change is our glorification—God's action in allowing us to share the glory and reward of heaven (see Rom. 8:17, 30).

Paul reminded the Philippians and us that "our citizenship is in heaven" (3:20a). This means that *now*, in this life, we are only temporary pilgrims; whereas *later*, in heaven, we will be eternal residents.

READINESS

Jesus Christ is coming again! Sometimes called the "Second Coming," the "Day of the Lord," or the "return of Christ," this truth is the sure promise of God the Father and the continuing hope of all who believe in him.

GOD PREPARES HIS PEOPLE

I teach a Bible study to inmates in the State Penitentiary of New Mexico. Our study began just over a year ago using materials developed by the Community Bible Study program. Our first study was the Gospel of John. After completing the study, the final lesson asked this question: "What is your favorite verse in the book and why?"

As we discussed this question, we were surprised to find that none of us had chosen the same verse. Most of the inmates are young enough to be my sons, and most of them selected verses that encouraged them as new and growing believers. They were surprised to learn that I had selected John 14:1–4, with particular emphasis on verse 2. To their queries I explained that the passage represented where I am in life, as did theirs. They need encouragement; I need promises. After being in the Lord's service for more than forty years, I find myself relishing reminders of God's promises related to my transition from this life/world to the next. To be sure, I am still on mission with God, but my "crossing over" draws nearer by the day. So, I am comforted by my Lord's words (as translated by Eugene Peterson[2]):

> Don't let this throw you. You trust God,
> don't you? Trust me. There is plenty of room for
> you in my Father's house. If it weren't so, would
> I have told you that I'm on my way to get your
> room ready for you? And if I'm on my way to

get your room ready, I'll come back and get you
so you can live where I live. And you already
know the road I'm taking. (John 14:1–4, *The
Message*)

I am delighted and thankful that God has taken the
initiative to prepare a place for me. What will it be like?
I don't know, but it will be perfect! I realize that I do not
deserve what he has prepared, and I assuredly have not
earned it. But Jesus certainly earned it for me! My
"room" in my Father's house is a gift of love and grace.
However, I have chosen to receive Jesus as my Lord and
Savior, and I have willingly and gratefully given him my
sins. So you see, there is a bit of human responsibility in
this heavenly commencement.

Human Readiness

I shudder to think of coming to my own death event
or to Jesus' second coming unprepared. Indeed, ample
admonitions are given by God to remind us to be ready
for either of these events.

In Jesus' parable of the rich man and the beggar
(Luke 16:19–31), we may glean these teachings:

1. Both men apparently entered their future conditions immediately following physical death.
2. The beggar's destination was a conscious state of
   blessedness; the rich man's destination was a state

of conscious torment. Jesus called the former state "Abraham's side" (16:22) and the latter he called "hell" (16:23).

3. Implicit in the parable is that one's attitude toward God, revealed in the actions of this life, determines one's destination (state) in the life to come. Thus, righteousness will be rewarded, and unrighteousness will be punished.[3]

To be ready to meet God, we must know the distinctions illustrated in this parable.

Matthew gives us the most extensive of Jesus' utterances about the end of the age (chaps. 24 and 25). The other synoptic Gospel writers give more abbreviated accounts (Mark 13:1–37 and Luke 21:5–36). A review of all these passages reveals several recurring warnings that are our calls to readiness: (1) Watch! (2) Be alert! (3) Be on guard! (4) Stand firm! (5) Do not worry! (6) Pray!

Because we do not know the time of Christ's return, we must maintain a constant vigil and preparedness. Jesus' parable of the ten virgins (Matt. 25:1–13) demonstrates this most poignantly: those who are not ready when the Bridegroom comes will be left behind!

God's good and faithful servants will maintain constant readiness—for their own physical death and for Messiah's return.

PRACTICAL DECISIONS

Though our spiritual readiness for death is by far the most important aspect of our very beings, our death also impacts our survivors. Accordingly, several important decisions should be addressed *before* we die.

THE RIGHT TO KNOW

Should you contract a terminal illness whose prognosis is imminent death, would you want to know? The issues associated with this question have precipitated considerable controversy and "game-playing," all of which seem to me unnecessarily tragic. To illustrate, the dying person may refuse to enter into a discussion of his impending death. He pretends indifference or feigns euphoria when in reality he is too frightened to broach the subject or allow another to do so. On the other hand, the terminally-ill person may view herself as needing to be stoic for the sake of her loved ones. Though she may wish to talk about dying, her decision to refrain is to protect others.

To eliminate these possibilities, I recommend that you reflect on the question, pray about your answer, and then tell those who need to know (your family, your physician, your pastor, etc.) what your wishes are. Such a courageous decision will help make your last days the best that they can be, and it will teach these others that pretense serves no one well.

While I have a strong personal preference regarding this issue, I know several others of the opposite ilk, and I respect their preference. Just as we have the right to choose whether we want to know (or not know) of our impending death, our next of kin needs to know our wishes. Let's tell them; the sooner, the better!

THE RIGHT TO DIE

Can you envision any possible contingencies in your life in which you would wish to allow your own death? If you thought the previous question was tough, this one is much tougher.

Earlier in this chapter I said, "We do not orchestrate our own death." While this statement represents my conviction, I must also say that years ago I executed a Living Will, in which I expressed my wish for a form of passive euthanasia *in the event of certain specific contingencies.* Let me explain this apparent inconsistency.

Euthanasia is commonly known today as mercy killing. From the Greek, *eu thanatos,* it literally means "good or easy death." The original meaning was possibly influenced by the death of Socrates (c. 400 B.C.). The revered philosopher and teacher drank hemlock and died a "noble" death (or so it is interpreted by some).

Today, the right-to-die issue revolves around the notion of passive versus active euthanasia. The former term means to *allow* death, while the latter term means to *cause* death. Proponents of the former decry *artificial life*—they disallow artificial life-sustaining treatments (e.g., respirators, feeding tubes, etc.) under certain conditions. These conditions are usually in circumstances involving irreversible terminal illness or an illness for which there would be no quality of life and for which attending physicians have said recovery is remote. A living will or a directive to physicians allows the person to either refuse or discontinue "heroic" methods to prolong life under those circumstances.

Proponents of active euthanasia are those who are more like Socrates (who calmly drank the poison) or those who request a physician to assist them in terminating their life. Most of us remember the work of Dr. Jack Kevorkian, who introduced what has come to be called physician-assisted suicide.

In chapter 5, I mentioned the term *health care surrogate,* a person appointed by another to interpret the latter's intentions regarding the withholding of life-sustaining procedures under certain stated contingencies. Both my wife and I have named each other and then our three sons, in succession, to be our health care surrogates. Our primary motive for this decision lies in our asking the question with which I began this section. As we wrestled with answering the question, we determined that should a situation develop in which we could only be kept alive artificially, we wanted to decide what would be done. Our decision was for our family more than for ourselves. Above all, we are trusting that our decisions are God-pleasing.

Funeral Arrangements

Of all persons who attend a funeral, for whom is that service most meaningful? Let me put this question differently: Is a funeral service for the deceased, or is it for all the others who attend? Is it helpful, or even appropriate, for a person to provide suggestions for any of an array of decisions associated with his/her own funeral?

It seems that more and more folks are writing out a proposed funeral service and giving it to their family with a request that it be used or at least considered when they die. It seems also that an increasing number of folks are opting for cremation, with either the scattering of their ashes or an inurnment—the burial of an urn containing their ashes.

As with the other matters we have discussed in this chapter, the chief requirement for effecting any of these important decisions is communication. The best solution for working through thorny issues, especially if the topic is considered by some to be taboo, is to bring them out into the open for discussion.

When death comes suddenly and without warning, the family members often experience shock. This makes funeral preparation difficult, but the planning is much easier if some arrangements have already been made. I recommend that you take the initiative in such preplanning. Ask your family how they feel about you making some of the arrangements. If they are amenable, then discuss those issues that are important to you: the funeral or memorial service, whether a burial plot has been secured, how they feel about an open or a closed casket, whether funds have been set aside for the various expenses, and the like.

If you or your spouse is a veteran, both of you are entitled to be buried in a national cemetery. Should this be your option, find out now what information and documentation will be needed to have you either interred or inurned.

A funeral is for survivors: family, friends, and acquaintances. While it affords an opportunity for the deceased to leave behind a final word of testimony, to request the singing or playing of a particular song, or to have a favorite Scripture read, the lasting effects of the service will be for those who have come to say good-bye. Because it is primarily for them, it is a good idea to query them about their preferences. It will be very important for your loved ones to receive what they will need for inspiration, for closure, and for a beginning (or continuation) of healing. All of these things are part of the grief work that each must do.

I hope we all can see that something as personal as death is really not a private affair. Few of us would wish to die alone. Rather, we prefer the comfort, love, and support of family and friends. Despite the "unknowns" of the next life, God's promises should be certain to us. Let us therefore rejoice and celebrate—even in the face of bereavement.

Jesus told his disciples, "In a little while you will see me no more, and then after a little while you will see me . . . . [Y]ou will weep and mourn . . . . You will grieve, but your grief will turn to joy" (John 16:19b–20). Was Jesus serious about this promise? My question is rhetorical for I know that you know the answer!

QUESTIONS FOR DISCUSSION

1. Do you feel that death is a taboo topic today for most older people that you know? How would you describe typical feelings about death and dying?

2. If you could exercise a preference regarding your own death (i.e., if God gave you a choice), what would it be? Would your choice be selfish or would it take into account the impact on others?

3. What is your current state of readiness for your own death and for the Messiah's second coming?

4. If you had a terminal illness, how easy or difficult would it be for your physician or family to keep that fact

from you if you refused to discuss it? Would you care at all about the feelings of these others?

5. Funeral services today contain many cultural and subcultural expectations. Reflect on some of these. How important are they to you? How important are they to others? Are they are worth discussing with family and friends? If they are worth discussing, who should take the initiative?

Appendix A
DEBUNKING THE MYTHS[1]

Myth 1: Senility Inevitably Accompanies Old Age

This myth is part of the conventional view that aging brings with it a decline in intelligence, memory, and learning. Yet empirical evidence shows that these relationships are quite complex, and decline is anything but inevitable. Age-related changes in learning ability appear to be quite small, even after the keenness of the senses has begun to decline. Memory and learning are functions of the central nervous system. Thus, when there is impairment, it is often due to some disease (arteriosclerosis, for example) or an associated condition. We should not assume that some typical process of normal aging is at work.

Myth 2: Most Old People Are Isolated from Their Families

Contrary to this myth, Marvin Sussman (1965) has argued that "there exists in modern urban-industrial societies an extended kin system made up of numerous nuclear families that exchange services and are partially dependent on each other."

More recently, Sussman (1976) observed that the proliferation of services for the elderly, such as Medicare and nutrition programs, has brought additional contact within families as relatives act as mediators between institutional bureaucracies and elderly family members.

MYTH 3: THE MAJORITY OF OLD PEOPLE ARE IN POOR HEALTH

I recently asked a group of third-year medical students what proportion of older people did they believe are sick and institutionalized. The consensus was that more than half of the older population are in ill health, and perhaps half of that population (25 percent of the total) are in institutions. *This simply is not the case.*

The majority of older people do *not* have the kinds of health problems that limit their ability to be employed or manage their own households, and only about 5 percent of those sixty-five and over can be found in an old-age institution on a given day. In a recent household-interview survey of the noninstitutionalized population, 67 percent of the older persons surveyed reported their own health as "good" or "excellent" in comparison with "others of their own age." Only 11 percent reported themselves as being in poor health.

MYTH 4: OLD PEOPLE ARE MORE LIKELY THAN YOUNGER PEOPLE TO BE VICTIMIZED BY CRIME

Concerns about crime against elderly Americans are quite high—especially among elderly Americans. Many surveys show that older persons are more fearful of crimes than are younger persons. This concern appears to stem from the popular belief that elderly persons are victimized more often than others and suffer more serious consequences as a result. Nevertheless, no evidence supports this belief.

National and local surveys show that the elderly are actually *less* likely to be victimized in all crime categories than are younger persons.

MYTH 5: THE MAJORITY OF OLD PEOPLE LIVE IN POVERTY

Many private and public programs have been developed in recent decades to deal with the economic problems of old age. According to James H. Schulz (1992) of Brandeis University, these programs include the following:

1. Substantial increases in Social Security old-age benefits in the last fifteen years (a faster rate of climb than inflation in the same period)
2. The growth of private pension plans with increased benefit levels
3. The creation of public health insurance and nutrition programs

4. The legislation of property tax and other tax relief laws in virtually all states

5. The Supplemental Security Income program (SSI), which now covers more than twice as many low-income elderly as did the now abolished old-age assistance plan, and raises benefit levels above previous levels of old-age assistance

MYTH 6: OLD PEOPLE TEND TO BECOME MORE RELIGIOUS AS THEY AGE

Religion serves a variety of functions in human societies. It functions both to maintain social control and to provide social support in times of need.

Do these functions change over time, as individuals and their families age and move through individual and developmental periods? Much research supports the lifetime stability model (Levin, 1989): . . . *organizational* religious involvement, such as attendance at religious services, is stable over the life course . . . *nonorganizational* religious involvement, such as watching religious television shows or praying at home, remains stable as people age, with some slight chance of increase among the very old and disabled to offset declines in organizational involvement.

MYTH 7: OLDER WORKERS ARE LESS PRODUCTIVE THAN YOUNGER ONES

This myth, based on misconceptions about the aging process and the employment of older people, is often raised by proponents of mandatory retirement. This argument assumes that older persons as a group may be less well suited for work than are younger workers because older people do not learn new skills as well as younger persons do, older workers are more inflexible with respect to changes in work schedules and regimens, and declining physical and mental capacities are found in greater proportion among older persons.

These arguments are not based on fact. Many studies indicate that older workers produce a quality of work equal or superior to that of younger workers. In addition, as we have already indicated, there is no reason to expect a decline in intellectual capacities with age, and there is every reason to assume that older workers in good health are capable of learning new skills when circumstances require it. Many workers can continue to work effectively beyond age sixty-five and may be better employees than younger workers because of greater experience and job commitment.

MYTH 8: OLD PEOPLE WHO RETIRE USUALLY SUFFER A DECLINE IN HEALTH AND AN EARLY DEATH

It is widely believed that retirement has an adverse effect on health. Most of us have heard at least one story about a retiree who "went downhill fast." The story usually describes an individual who carefully plans for retirement, only to become sick and die within a brief period of time.

One problem with such stories is that the health status of the retiree before retirement is never made clear. Another problem is that most retirees themselves are older, and, although the majority of older people do not have major health problems, it is true that older people have a greater risk of illness than do younger people. *Health declines appear to be associated with age, not with retirement!*

MYTH 9: MOST OLD PEOPLE HAVE NO INTEREST IN, OR CAPACITY FOR, SEXUAL RELATIONS

Sexual interests, capacities, and functions change with age. Nevertheless, older men and women in reasonably good health can have an active and satisfying sex life.

Older people need not duplicate the sexual behavior of youth in order to enjoy their sexual experiences. Sex is qualitatively different in the later years. Sexual activity in later years may fulfill the human need for the warmth of physical closeness and the intimacy of companionship. Older people should be encouraged to seek this fulfillment.

MYTH 10: MOST OLD PEOPLE END UP IN NURSING HOMES AND OTHER LONG-TERM CARE INSTITUTIONS

Most old people do *not* end up in nursing homes. The 1990 census reports* that about 5 percent of the elderly population resides in old-age institutions of one kind or another. Still, this does not mean that the odds of being institutionalized are one in twenty. The census gives us a picture of the institutional population at one point in time.

* Current reports are quite similar.

Appendix B
SUGGESTIONS FOR HOW TO EAT[1]

1. *Eat only when you are hungry.* This may seem obvious, but think about it for awhile; in fact, think about it every time you feel like eating. When you feel like eating, decide if you are really hungry or not. If you are, wait ten minutes before you get something to eat. Don't eat simply because the clock tells you it's time for a meal.

2. *Stop eating when you can still eat a little more.* (If you wish to linger at the table, have a cup of tea or a glass of club soda or mineral water—all of which are calorie-free—and sip it slowly.)

3. *When you are at home, eat at one place only.* Pick out your favorite seat at the dining room or kitchen table and sit there every time you eat, even if you are only eating an apple. Never eat when you are standing.

4. *Eat as slowly as you can.* A meal should take at least twenty minutes; a snack, ten minutes. Your brain

needs time to receive the message that you have eaten. Chew slowly and think about how the food tastes. It helps to put your fork or spoon down between bites instead of using it like a shovel.

5. *Don't read or watch TV when eating.* Concentrate on eating and on conversation when you eat with someone else.

6. *Use a smaller size plate* (salad or luncheon plate), so that usual portions of food appear generous.

7. *Don't leave snack food around in inviting dishes throughout your home.* Keep all foods in one room, out of sight in cupboards or in the refrigerator, when you are not eating.

8. *Practice leaving a little food on your plate.* You really don't have to eat it all, even if that's your usual style.

9. *Always eat three meals a day.* Don't skip a meal because you want to "splurge" later; just eat a little less. *Never* skip breakfast.

NOTES

CHAPTER ONE

1. Cary S. Kart, *The Realities of Aging,* fourth edition (Needham Heights: Allyn and Bacon, 1994).

CHAPTER TWO

1. Kart, *The Realities of Aging,* 7.
2. Ibid.
3. Robert Butler, quoted in ibid., 2.

CHAPTER THREE

1. The National Council on the Aging, Inc., *Retirement Planning Program* (Washington, D.C., 1979–88), 85–86.
2. Ibid., 85.
3. Barbara Deane, *Getting Ready for a Great Retirement* (Colorado Springs: NavPress, 1992), 202.

CHAPTER FOUR

1. Kart, *The Realities of Aging,* 185.
2. L. Noelker and Z. Harel, quoted in ibid., 439.

CHAPTER FIVE

1. James F. Fries and Lawrence M. Crapo, *Vitality and Aging* (San Francisco: W. H. Freeman and Company, 1981), 3.

2. The National Council on the Aging, Inc., *Retirement Planning Program*, 15–16.

3. Ibid., 76.

4. Ibid.

CHAPTER NINE

1. Jodie E. Yoder, "Ugly Gremlins," *Our Daily Bread*, 5 September 2001.

2. David H. Roper, "Old Timers," *Our Daily Bread*, 13 December 2001.

3. Dale Gallagher, "Am I Too Old?" *Mature Living*, September 2001, 45.

CHAPTER TEN

1. *NIV Disciple's Study Bible* (Nashville: Holman Bible Publishers, 1988), 1,735.

2. Eugene Peterson, *The Message* (Colorado Springs: NavPress, 1995).

3. *NIV Disciple's Study Bible*, 1,296.

APPENDIX A

1. Kart, *The Realities of Aging*, 7–15.

APPENDIX B

1. Annette Natow and Jo-Ann Heslin, *Nutrition for the Prime of Your Life* (New York: McGraw-Hill Book Company, 1983), 157–58.